A Few
Essential Disciplines
of the
Christ Follower

This book identifies a short list of specific spiritual disciplines. The author identifies and defines each. Further, he provides supportive Scripture references with each. He considers these disciplines to be special. He considers them to be essential.

The origin of this book is his own experience as a disciple. You will get somewhat acquainted with Jim as you read. It is as if you are reading his journal. This is personal for him, as he writes about his victories and his failures. You will sense his sincerity. You will appreciate his candor and integrity. His explanation of doctrine is his own, identifying himself as a student with much to learn.

This author's goal is to identify these essential disciplines for you. In so doing he wants to encourage you, as a disciple of Christ, to practice these disciplines in your walk with the Lord.

Michael T Sanders

Adjunct Professor
Congregational Ministry
Johnson University

Jim's life has been one on assignment from God. This newest assignment, with practical advice from years of faithfulness, is a roadmap of spiritual exercises that will keep you on the path of Christ-like growth and transformation. Follow them and you will finish strong.

Ed Berry

Pastor
Henry Christian Church

Table of Contents

Introduction

Something I enjoyed doing for many years is discipling new Christians. It all began several years after I became a Christian. I was about 30 years old and doing business in Louisville Ky. A good friend and business partner invited me to have lunch at the Galt House Hotel. He told me it would be sponsored by the **Christian Businessmen's Committee (CBMC)** of Louisville. I was not familiar with them at all and really did not know what to expect.

There must have been 200 businessmen there sitting at round tables eating lunch while listening to a professional athlete give his testimony about becoming a Christian. At the end of the talk an invitation was given for anyone who wanted to talk to someone about their faith. On each table there was a card to fill out regarding your decision. Also, on the card was a place to check if you were already a Christian and would be interested in discipling someone who had accepted Christ at the luncheon.

Something prompted me to check that box and in several weeks I was contacted by a gentleman who wanted to meet with me to discuss my response. It turns out that CBMC was a well-organized global ministry with chapters in nearly every major city in the United States.

He explained to me that when someone during lunch checked the box that indicated they had decided to ask Jesus to be their Savior, they then would be contacted by a mentor to help them solidify their decision and to take them through a discipling program. He asked me if I would want to be a mentor. I agreed and was given a tool to use called "Operation Timothy". I would meet with the man, help him solidify his decision to become a Christian, talk with him*** about baptism and church, and finally to go through the Operation Timothy course. The course would help the new Christian understand how to live the Christian life.

Operation Timothy has both a leader and student guide. The guide has 13 chapters which you try to cover in 13 weeks. It requires meeting once every week to review a chapter. The student would also have to memorize a scripture verse that went along with the lesson.

Over the years I began discipling in other settings, such as Southeast Christian Church in Louisville Ky. I eventually developed my own guide that only took 6 weeks. I found that in today's busy world it was hard for men to commit to 13 weeks which usually turned into 6 months when you figured in vacations, illnesses, and prior commitments. The shorter time seemed to be more manageable. In this guide I provide 6 disciplines that I have come to believe are especially important to someone who is serious about living a Christian life.

I find it interesting, that as I am writing this book, the world is going through one of the toughest times I can ever remember in my life. We have been attacked by a coronavirus that has been named Covid19. Our government has had to shut down all non-essential business and gatherings as well as put in place guidelines for social distancing. All this has been done for our protection. One of the biggest challenges through this process has been to determine what businesses and gatherings are essential to our survival. Obviously, things like food markets, hospitals, gas stations, etc. have had to be considered essential.

As we have been going through this pandemic we have also been dealing with political division like never before and civil unrest including protests and rioting. I have decided to add a chapter at the end of the book about the virus and the reaction of people across our country as it has affected our relationship with God and each other. In the same chapter I will also explore how we use our Christian disciplines to help us through times such as this.

I began to think how ironic it was that I would be writing this book at the time we are experiencing all this. As we begin the Christian life I have found that we make some drastic changes. We should also begin doing some things that help us mature as Christians. We could call these new practices disciplines. We could call some of the important one's essential disciplines.

I asked myself, "what are some essential disciplines we should incorporate into our walk with God?"

The six I have chosen are basic to the Christ follower. We learn them through the guidance of the Holy Spirit, attending church, taking part in bible studies, and watching how other mature Christians live their lives. If the Christ follower does not begin to see the need for these basic routines in their life, it might be time to do a heart check. They should examine themselves to see if there has been true change in the heart as brought about by the guidance of the Holy Spirit. Acts 2:38 says.

" *Repent and be baptized, every one of you, in the name of Jesus Christ for the forgiveness of your sins. And you will receive the gift of the Holy Spirit. The promise is for you and your children and all who are far off - for all whom the Lord our God will call.*"

I would not want anybody who reads this to think that I am saying, if you are not participating in these disciplines that you are not a Christian or any less of a Christian. Only God knows a person's heart and He is the ultimate Judge. I think doing these things should be part of becoming a more mature and committed Christ follower .

Disciplines are part of the sanctification process. Sanctification is the theological term for becoming more like Jesus.

I am writing this book in hopes that there are others who might benefit from implementing these disciplines in their own life. These disciplines not only drew me closer to the Lord throughout my life, but they also helped me try to live the life that God wants His children to live.

I would also like to say to the reader that the ideas that I put forth and the scriptures I use are ones I felt led to use based on my study and convictions. I recommend that you study each scripture and wrestle with each idea, as you ask God to help you know the truth. Jesus said in John 8:31-3

"If you accept my teachings and become my disciples, then you will know the truth and the truth will set you free."

Chapter 1
Becoming a Christ Follower
And sharing our faith

I have found in life that we should be careful about assuming things. It probably would not be fair to assume that every person who stumbles across this book has become a Christian. If you find yourself in that situation I would like to take the time in this first chapter to offer you an opportunity to become one. I fear that without taking that step you would have a difficult time understanding or embracing the disciplines we will be discussing.

Some people have no desire to follow this path and in fact never give it a thought. They have come to a place where they believe there is no God. Others however have given it thought but for different reasons have not followed through. Maybe you have developed the idea that it is too difficult? Maybe you think you must give up too much? One of the most common reasons people hesitate is they feel they have done too much wrong in their life. Maybe you are thinking I need to clean myself up or make myself presentable so that God will accept me? None of this is true. In fact, God wants us to come to Him just as we are.

I am reminded of a hymn that was played every time the great evangelist Billy Graham offered an invitation. The name of the hymn was "Just as I Am."

You might be surprised when you find out how easy it is to become a Christian. Sure, it seems hard and for a good reason. Everything in this world is screaming for you not to do it. In fact, we all have an adversary who is really the opposite of God. In the Bible he is referred to as Satan. He is also referred to as the prince of this world and the prince of darkness. He knows that when we give our lives to God we become a part of the kingdom of God. At that point Satan loses a great battle. I know this all sounds farfetched, but it is all true. To tell you the truth not only is Satan against us becoming a child of God but much of this world is against us as well. So, you need to understand that when you are trying to make your mind up to become one of God's children there is a battle going on for your soul. That may be why it seems so difficult.

I have met many people who have decided to take a neutral position. They feel that they will just not take sides and when they die it will be a nonevent. Their body will melt back into the goo that the earth was made of. I wish I could accommodate that thinking but it is not at all what God's word teaches.

In Matthew 12:30 Jesus says

" *whoever is not with me is against me.*"

It is impossible to be neutral about Jesus Christ. Anyone who is not actively following him has chosen a path leading away from him. Any person who tries to remain neutral in the struggle of good against evil is choosing to be separated from God, who alone is good. To refuse to follow Jesus is to choose to be on his opponent's side.

Over the years I have had the privilege to help a few people as they have come to the point they felt they needed to turn to God. I discovered several ways to make the process a little easier to understand and work through. By the way I would like to say at this point that the thing that happens to a person during this process has been given several names. The most common you will hear is "being saved". Sometimes you might also hear "being born again" or "being baptized". Some denominations have a process called "confirmation". Usually in this tradition you are baptized as a baby and when you reach an age when you can determine on your own you would like to be a part of the Church, you go through classes such as catechism. I have a friend who is Catholic that explained to me the way their confirmation works. It is considered a Sacrament and takes place in a ceremony that allows a person who is baptized as a baby to later confirm their faith and receive the gifts of the Holy Spirit by the laying of hands and anointing with holy oils by the bishop.

You might be asking yourself, "being saved from what?" That is a good question.

I am now going to share with you one of the ways that I learned to help people walk through the process of being saved and as I do it will help you understand what you are being saved from. Many of these thoughts and illustrations I learned as a decision guide at Southeast Christian Church.

Before we get started I want to share a short story with you. I learned early on that the best way to help someone who is searching is to tell them what God has done for me.

When my mother was seventeen she lived in Frankfort, KY. She found herself pregnant with me and not married. That was not a very accepted thing in 1953. She had decided to get an abortion. Back then they did not have clinics; they had what was called midwives. She went to a midwife's house. The midwife had her get up on a table, gave her a glass of whiskey to drink, and left the room. My mother got scared and ran out of the house. Being homeless at the time, she wandered around town that evening, until she found an abandoned car. After climbing into the back seat and going to sleep, she dreamed that she heard angels singing. The next day she decided not to have an abortion.

I was never fortunate enough to know my father. When I was three or four years old my mother married a military man. He moved us around the country to places like Norfolk, Philadelphia, and Newport R.I. One half-sister and two half-brothers later, we found ourselves in Great Lakes, Ill.

This man became an alcoholic and was very abusive. He would beat my mother and me. When I was 13, he had beaten me to the point of death for the second time. My mother found the courage to leave him. She went to the Commander of the base and reported his actions. The Commander forced him to relocate us back to Frankfort and to give her a divorce.

At the age of fourteen, I found myself pretty much on my own. I eventually fell into the wrong crowd. I started smoking cigarettes and drinking alcohol. I also started stealing. At first it was just shoplifting, but soon I graduated to things like car stereo systems. I got involved with some older men, who taught me how to steal cars. I also had started smoking marijuana regularly. By eighteen I was doing LSD and whatever else I could get my hands on. You talk about a messed-up life, and it gets more interesting. I met a beautiful girl named Debbie. She did not know everything about me. After going together for two years we got married, and she gave birth to my son James Jr. I was still doing bad things. When she had her fill of me staying messed up on drugs and not coming home for days, she took my son and moved back home with her parents. I ended up hooked on a drug called Mescaline. One morning I woke up in a trailer laying in my own vomit. I had been high on Mescaline for 2 weeks. Something told me to get up and get out of there.

I hitchhiked to Louisville to see if my wife would consider giving me another chance.

Much to my surprise she did. Currently, I had absolutely nothing to my name.

For the next few years, I worked for several companies doing heating and air-conditioning, a trade I had learned from my father-in-law. I eventually ended up in a job working with a man named Hilliard Vincent. All this time I had never really gotten straightened out. I was kind of living two lives. Hilliard was mentioning things to me about God that I had never realized. You see, Hilliard was a Christian and he was witnessing to me, only I did not realize it. One day when I had reached about as low as I could go, I called Hilliard. He said he had been waiting for me to call. I asked if he would meet with me. He had me meet him at his church that evening. It was a little Missionary Baptist Church. No one was there except Hilliard and me. He turned on just enough lights for us to make our way to the altar. I explained to him how I felt that there had to be more to life, or it was not worth living any more. He told me about Jesus. I asked him what I needed to do. He showed me some different scripture's and explained the plan of salvation to me. Then he led me in the prayer of confession, and I asked Jesus to come into my life. I remember telling him that I did not feel anything happen. He said not to worry, that what I had done, I had done in faith, and I would see some changes.

My life has never been the same!

I began to see many changes. I graduated from Louisville Technical Institute with a degree in Mechanical Design. Some men approached me about starting a business doing commercial heating air conditioning and plumbing. I agreed to do it, and so in 1980 a company called J&J Mechanical was born. I dedicated that business to the Lord. By this time, my wife and I had a little girl named Jenny. So, J&J was named after our children James and Jenny. After being active in the Cumberland Presbyterian Church for several years, I decided to enter the ministry part time. I enrolled in the alternate studies program at Memphis Theological Seminary. I graduated in 1985 and was ordained.

So much has happened in the last 40 years it is hard to believe. God has opened so many doors. My wife and I have been married now for 48 years. My son has become a successful entrepreneur in Los Angeles and owns his own computer company. My daughter, who became a schoolteacher, has provided us with a handsome grandson who is 25 now. My wife and I have both served as President of Wayside Christian Mission in Louisville. The Lord gave me a gift of helping run Christian ministries. After serving several years on the board of Wayside Christian mission I spent 5 years as chairman of the board of Greater Louisville Youth for Christ. After that some men approached me about a Christian School in Shelbyville that was struggling to stay in business.

I spent 5 years as its chairman of the board and was able to get a facility built. I started a development company called JIL (Jesus is Lord) Dev. We built residential subdivisions. My wife started a house building company called DK Builders. We eventually sold J&J Mechanical to a company in Texas and it is now on the NYSE. God has allowed me to travel the world from the Holy Land in Israel to doing mission work in South America.

Along the way I was doing so much traveling that I had to get my pilot's license. We have owned several airplanes and used them to do Angel Flights. That is a program where I flew sick children to hospitals and clinics around the country. One of my favorite things was serving as a Minister on call and Decision guide at Southeast Christian church in Louisville Ky.

It is amazing what God can do!

Mark 8:36 asks the question,

"What would it profit a man if he were to gain the whole world and lose his own soul"?

Sharing with someone what God has done for you sets the stage to be able to share what we refer to as the plan of salvation.

One of the important things we must accept as we start this journey of becoming a Christian and living the Christian life is that we did not evolve but that we were created by God. This is hard for us because we are taught from childhood in school that we evolved. We must accept by faith that we were created. We will talk about faith many times in this book. Hebrews 11:1 says that.

"Faith is the substance of things hoped for and the evidence of things not seen.

Do not expect God to prove himself to you personally before you place your faith in him. Jesus says in John 20:29.

"Blessed are those who believe without seeing me"

We have all the miracles recorded in the Old and New Testaments, 2,000 years of church history, and the witness all around us of thousands who have been saved, reconciled, rehabilitated, and healed by God. With all this evidence, those who will not believe are either too proud or too stubborn. If you simply step forward in faith and believe, then you will begin to see the miracles that God can do in your life and is doing in the lives of others!

The question then becomes why God created us. Have you ever asked yourself questions like "Why am I here? Why do I exist? What is my purpose? What is the thing I was made to do?"

There are some people who appear to wander around aimlessly; however, I think most of us do search for meaning.

The Bible teaches us that God created us to glorify Him, to know Him, and to enjoy life in Him forever.

How do we glorify God?

Isaiah 6:3 says that *"the whole earth is full of His glory."*

Psalms 19:1 says, *"the heavens declare the glory of God."*

Romans 3:23 says *"we all fall short of the glory of God"*

1 Corinthians 10:31 says *"whatever we do , do it all for the glory of God."*

So, you must ask yourself, Is the way I am living bringing glory to God?

How do we know God? We know God when we know Jesus. Jesus said that when you have seen Him you have seen the Father (God), because He and the Father (God) are one. This brings us to one of the first tests of faith. One of the hardest things for me to overcome was to believe in something I could not see. When I decided by faith to ask Jesus to come into my heart, I began to see some changes in myself. I learned that my confession of faith allowed God's spirit to enter me which caused me to sense the presence of God in my mind.

The more that I yield myself to the prompting I sense from God's spirit and the more I talk to Him in my mind, the more I get to know Him.

Who does not want to enjoy life? The fact is that most people who are searching are not enjoying life as much as they could.

In the Old Testament Jeremiah 29:11 says,

"I know the plans I have for you declares the Lord, "plans to prosper" you and not to harm you, plans to give you hope and a future."

Jesus said in the New Testament in John 10:10

"I have come that you might have life and have it more abundantly."

I can honestly say that I have enjoyed the last 40 years as a child of God so much more than my first 27 years searching for happiness in the things of this world.

But…

There is a problem. We have all sinned against God (disobeyed Him). From the beginning of humanity man has turned his back on God. Romans 3:23 says, *"all have sinned and fallen short of the glory of God."*

God created us in His own image to have an abundant life. He did not make us as robots to automatically love and obey Him but gave us a will and a freedom of choice. We chose to disobey God and go our own way. We still make this choice today. This results in separation from God.

In this illustration we get a visual of what separation from God looks like.

You can see that there is like a large canyon between us and God. In our sinful lost condition, there is no way for us to reach Him. This sin that separates us from God causes our eternal death. Romans 6:23 says,

" The wages of sin are death."

How can we be reconciled with God? How can we bridge the canyon and make things right with our creator? Many have tried various ways to get across the canyon. We talked about how people were not enjoying life. You read in my story how I tried different things to find happiness and could not find it.

This 2nd illustration shows some of the ways that the world has tried to bridge the gap between man and God.

You can see that being a person of high morals and doing a lot of good work will not get you there. You can also see that practicing religions of different kinds or being a great philosopher will not get you there either.

Proverbs 14:12 says,

"there is a way that seems right to man but in the end it leads to death and destruction."

What can we do?

This 3rd illustration shows us what God's solution to our problem looks like.

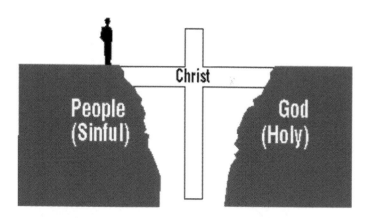

God provided a way for us. His remedy was Jesus. God had a son named Jesus whom He sent into this world. He allowed His son to die on a cross for us to bridge the gap.

John 3:16 says.

"God so loved the world that He gave His only begotten son, that whoever believes in him shall not perish but have eternal life."

And He did this while we were still in sin! Romans 5:8 says.

"God demonstrated His love for us in this: While we were yet sinners, Christ died for us."

You will learn through study that the way Jesus died for us was being hung on a cross. It is often referred to as the old, rugged cross. You can see in this illustration how the cross of Jesus became the bridge that has allowed us to get across the canyon to God.

You see there is only one true way to God, and it is through His son Jesus. Jesus said in John 14:6.

"I am the way the truth and the life, no one comes to the father except through me."

Acts 4:12 says.

"salvation is found in no one else, for there is no other name under heaven given to mankind by which we must be saved." (That name is Jesus.)

You see when Jesus died on that cross He shed His blood for us. God allowed that blood to be the sacrifice for our sin and the means by which we could be saved if we would only believe.

How do we get started? How do we allow Jesus into our heart?

1st. You must accept and believe the things I have shared with you. You do this by faith. In some ways it is like taking a leap of faith. It takes courage. You must silence those thoughts that are holding you back and listen to that voice that is beckoning you to say yes.

In Revelation 3:20 Jesus said.

"Behold I stand at the door and knock, if anyone hears my voice I will come in and eat with them, and they with me."

For me I had come to a point that I had tried everything else. I was feeling that there had to be something more and I was willing to give it a try even though everything in me was screaming "this doesn't make sense."

2nd. You must repent. What does it mean to repent? What are you repenting from? You are repenting from a life of rebellion and sin.

You might think repent simply means to be sorry. However, repenting is much more than just being sorry. It also means taking action. You must decide in your heart, mind, and soul that you are going to make changes. You are going to strive to not live the life you have been living and to live one that would bring glory to God. In some ways you are actually changing direction and going the opposite from the way you have been going.

Acts 3:19 says.

" Repent, then, and turn to God, so that your sins might be wiped out."

2nd Corinthians 7:10 says.

"Godly sorrow brings repentance that leads to salvation and leaves no regret."

3rd. You must make a confession. What does it mean to confess? Can you remember as a child doing something bad and having to admit you did it and then say you are sorry? Confession becomes an opportunity for you to talk to God for the first time and tell Him how you feel. You can admit to Him you have been rebellious. You can tell Him how sorry you are, ask Him to forgive you, and ask Him to become your Lord and Savior.

Romans 10:9 says.

"If you confess with your mouth that Jesus is Lord and believe in your heart that God raised Him from the dead, you will be saved."

4th. You need to be baptized. What does it mean to be baptized? In a nutshell I consider it a way to seal the deal. Jesus introduced Christian baptism by experiencing it Himself when He began His ministry. His cousin John had been preaching repentance. Jesus went to John and was baptized in the Jordan river. When that happened, a dove came down and a voice spoke.

Jesus' baptism is recorded in Mathew 3: 13-17.

"Then Jesus came from Galilee to the Jordan to be baptized by John. But John tried to deter him, saying, "I need to be baptized by you, and do you come to me? "Jesus replied, "Let it be so now; it is proper for us to do this to fulfill all righteousness." Then John consented. As soon as Jesus was baptized, he went up out of the water. At that moment heaven was opened, and he saw the Spirit of God descending like a dove and alighting on him. And a voice from heaven said, "This is my Son, whom I love; with him I am well pleased." My beloved son whom I love and with whom I am well pleased."*

I have learned that baptism is symbolic of the death, burial, and resurrection of Jesus.

When we are submerged in the water it represents us being buried with Christ and when we come up out of the water it represents us being raised to life. We are dying to our old self and being raised to a new life in Christ.

2nd Corinthians 5:17 says.

"if anyone is in Christ they are a new creation, the old is gone and the new has come."

Baptism is also a picture of our sins being washed away. It really becomes an outward sign of an inward change that we are experiencing.

Lastly it gives us an opportunity to tell the world that we are becoming a child of God and part of His kingdom.

Mathew 10:32 Jesus says,

"Whoever acknowledges me before others, I will also acknowledge them before me Father in heaven."

So, the big question now is are you ready to take this step?

If so you can do it wherever you are. It is just a matter of having a conversation with God. This is something you can do by yourself or with another Christian.

If you are by yourself and you are in a quiet place you could just kneel or get in a comfortable position and begin to talk to God. You can do this in your head under your breath or you can speak out loud. I spoke out loud my first time because I was with a friend.

I can help you now with a prayer that you could use in case you have a hard time thinking of what to say.

"Dear Lord, I know now that I have lived a life separated from you because of my sin. I believe that you died for my sins. I am asking you to forgive me of my sins. I want to repent and live my life for you. I ask you to come into my heart and be my Lord and Savior. I want to trust and follow you from this day forward."

"In Jesus' name I pray. Amen"

What happens after this prayer is different for everyone. Some have an emotional experience and others do not. I was one who did not. However, I will promise you, that if you said that prayer and meant it God will honor it. You will begin to see some changes in your life.

Ok, now that you have given your life to Christ you are going to need some help. I recommend that you find a friend who is a Christian and tell them what you have done.

Or you could find a Christian church and make arrangements to meet with a minister to discuss what you have done and learn what your next steps would be.

Warning!

I always warn folks that at this point that Satan does not give up. He wants to make you think that what you just did was not real. He wants to get you sidetracked.

1st Peter 5:8-9 says.

"Be alert and of sober mind. Your enemy the devil prowls around like a roaring lion looking for someone to devour. Resist him, standing firm in the faith..."

It is so important to talk to someone and share your experience with them as well as get plugged into a church. Another important thing you will want to do is talk to someone who can help you arrange for your baptism.

Now we have come to the point that we can begin learning about some of the disciplines of living the Christian life.

Before we leave this chapter I would like to discuss a discipline that we need to understand as we begin the life of a Christ Follower. That is the discipline of sharing our faith.

I think about the gift of salvation and how important it is for us to share that gift with others.

What if you had discovered you had cancer. What if you learned of a doctor who had a cure for the cancer you have? You went to that doctor and received treatments that cured you. You would be so happy. Then you found out about a friend who had the same cancer. Wouldn't you want to share with them the name of the doctor who treated you?

What if you were walking in your neighborhood and you saw smoke coming out of one of your neighbor's house. What if you knew they were home and maybe asleep? Wouldn't you do anything you could to go in and save them?

The truth is that someone who has never said yes to Jesus is in a much worse situation then if they were caught in a fire in their home or were dying of cancer.

Once you have been saved you have a lifeline to friends and family that are perishing because of being separated from God. The Holy Spirit living inside you will give you the burden for others that are still lost. When you receive that burden, you can go back and review this chapter to learn how to help them.

Chapter 2
Prayer

As we begin to study disciplines I want to make it clear that they do not make us a Christian. However, they can help us to become a more mature and committed Christian. Disciplines are the way we express our love for God and to fulfill the plans He has for us. We do them because we have been changed by the Holy Spirit. Each one serves a different purpose. Prayer is the way we communicate with God. Scripture reading is the way we learn about God. Memorizing scriptures protects us and gives us confidence. Attending church gives us the opportunity to worship God, participate in Holy Communion, and have an avenue to give. Giving is our response to God by sharing a part of what He has given us to further His Kingdom here on earth. Christian service is the way we become the hands and feet of God here on earth. All these disciplines help us in our sanctification, which again, is the process of becoming more like Jesus.

We never want to get the idea that these works we do save us or make us any better than anyone else. Salvation is not about being good, it is about faith. These works we do are a result of the change we experience after our faith has helped us to say yes to Jesus. The Bible teaches us that salvation does not come by our works but that works are a result of our salvation.

Eph 2:8-10

"It was by grace that you were saved through faith - and this is not of yourselves, it is a gift of God - not of works lest any man should boast."

" for we are God's handiwork, created in Christ Jesus to do good works, which God prepared in advance for us."

So, our works come after we are saved. Because of a changed heart we want to serve God with all that we have. I believe He already has in mind the things that He wants each of us to do.

As Jesus was doing his ministry here on earth and preparing humanity for the Kingdom of God, He had problems with several groups called the pharisees and Sadducees.

These Jewish leaders had taken the laws that God had given to Moses in the Old Testament and turned them into difficult traditions that were almost impossible for the people to live by. They even used prayer to be seen and heard in a way that was not pleasing to God. I like what Jesus said in Matthew 6: 5-8.

"And when you pray, do not be like the hypocrites, for they love to pray standing in the synagogues and on the street corners to be seen by others.

Truly I tell you, they have received their reward in full. But when you pray, go into your room, close the door, and pray to your Father, who is unseen. Then your Father, who sees what is done in secret, will reward you. And when you pray, do not keep on babbling like pagans, for they think they will be heard because of their many words. Do not be like them, for your Father knows what you need before you ask him."

When Jesus said these words, He was delivering the greatest sermon ever preached called the Sermon on the Mount.

This brings us to the first of several kinds of prayer we will be discussing. I consider this to be our basic prayer. In church today it is referred to as the Lord's Prayer. As Jesus was preaching this sermon He went on to say in Matthew 6: 9-14.

"This, then, is how you should pray:
*"**Our Father** in heaven,*
hallowed be your name,
your kingdom come,
your will be done, on earth as it is in heaven.
Give us today our daily bread.
And forgive us our sins,
as we forgive those who sin against us.
And lead us not into temptation,
but deliver us from the evil one."

Later the church added to the Lord's Prayer a doxology as follows.

"For thine is the kingdom, and power, and glory forever.

Amen."

When I was a young boy, every morning as school began, we would all stand up and say the Lord's prayer along with the pledge of allegiance to the flag. In later years, the Supreme Court would decide that it was unconstitutional to force children to say the Lord's prayer in school. About that same time, it was decided schools had to teach evolution.

As we continue with the various kinds of prayer I would like to emphasize that prayer is something we can and should do all the time.

The Apostle Paul said in 1st Thessalonians 5:17.

" Pray continually"

What does that look like? How can we do that? Here are some examples of how that works with me. I might be riding down the road noticing how beautiful things are and say, "thank you Lord for the beauty of your creation." I might be doing something and hurt myself and say, "Lord help this not to be bad."

When I am having bad thoughts, such as lust, judging others, anger, pride, jealousy, the list goes on, I catch myself and say, "help me Lord." Sometimes I might have to keep repeating "help me Lord" over and over until the thoughts disappear. The Bible refers to this as taking thoughts captive.

2 Corinthians 10:3-5 says.

"For though we live in the world, we do not wage war as the world does. The weapons we fight with are not the weapons of the world. On the contrary, they have divine power to demolish strongholds. We demolish arguments and every pretension thought that sets itself up against the knowledge of God, and we take captive every thought to make it obedient to Christ."

One question we may ask is "why do we pray?"

Our prayers may not change God's mind, but they may change ours. Prayer helps us better understand the mind of God.

There are numerous reasons to pray but I think one of the most important is that we pray for our own edification.

I am reminded of a story that a golf buddy of mine once told. His name is Dennis Long. We were on a golf trip and Dennis was asked to give a devotional.

He said it was important for him to continuously recharge his batteries through spending time with God. He had two cans of Coke. He held one in each hand. He squeezed the one in his left hand and it crushed. He squeezed the one in his right hand and could not crush it even when he squeezed it as hard as he could. He said he had put a pinhole in the one he crushed, and it was empty but the one that was still full he could not crush. He said he was like the can of Coke. The things of this world were always draining him of his joy. As he became emptier Satan could crush him. So, he tried to refill himself as he was being drained. He was filling himself with the Holy Spirit through spending time alone with God in prayer. I think there were other disciplines that probably helped him, such as, studying scripture and attending church.

We pray for the ones we love. For their edification, healing, and salvation among other things.

We pray for those we do not know because we are asked to, and they need our prayers for many different reasons. God even instructs us to pray for our enemies.

Prayer becomes the conversations we have with God like and ongoing dialog. I like to ask people, "how would you act if Jesus were sitting right beside you?" Well guess what? He is. God hears our every word and sees our every act.

It is always good to have a friend to talk to. Jesus can be that friend.

One of my favorite old hymns is " What a Friend We Have in Jesus." The lyrics go as follows.

What a friend we have in Jesus

All our sins and griefs to bear

What a privilege to carry

Everything to God in prayer

Oh, what peace we often forfeit

Oh, what needless pain we bear

All because we do not carry

Everything to God in prayer

Have we trials and temptations?

Is there trouble anywhere?

We should never be discouraged

Take it to the Lord in prayer.

You may be thinking "how does all of this work?" It all begins to make sense when you consider that you received God's spirit in you when you asked Christ to come into your heart and was baptized. Peter said in Acts 2:38-39.

"Repent and be baptized, every one of you, in the name of Jesus Christ for the forgiveness of your sins. And you will receive the gift of the Holy Spirit. The promise is for you and your children and for all who are far off—for all whom the Lord our God will call."

It is God's Spirit living in us that facilitates our being able to talk with Him. You may ask, "what is God's Spirit"? He is called the Holy Spirit. One concept that many people have trouble with is that God is three persons in one. We call it the Trinity. Although that term is not used in the Bible, it is a term established by the Church to describe God being three in one. Throughout the Bible we are taught that there is God the Father, God the Son, and God the Holy Spirit. When Jesus left the earth, He sent the Holy Spirit to us in a new way in which we could all have Him living in us. You may ask "how do I know He is in me"? The scripture above teaches us when we repent and are baptized we receive the Holy Spirit. Later in this chapter when I discuss praying in unknown languages, I share how I know the Holy Spirit is in me.

We know that He hears us when we pray because the Bible teaches us that He does. Even if He does not always answer the way we think He should, He still hears us. The Psalmist declared in Psalm 55:16-17.

"As for me, I call to God ... and he hears my voice"

From the beginning of the Old Testament to the end of the New Testament we read of God's people talking to Him and Him answering. He does not always give us the answer we want.

My friend Bob Russell said that sometimes God says "yes", sometimes He says "no", and sometimes He says, "not yet."

How do we hear God's answer?

For me there are several ways. I have never heard an audible voice as described by some in the Bible. That is not to say God could not still do that today, because God can do anything. I did hear a voice once when I was extremely ill. I was about 30 years old and a blood vessel ruptured in my stomach. I had been given about 20 units of blood in 3 days and was barely hanging on. As I drifted off to sleep for what I thought was the last time, I heard this voice say, "give up, give up". I immediately said, " Father take me to heaven". When I woke up 2 days later my wife was on one side and my mother-in-law was on the other side and I had a smile on my face.

I have also had several spiritual dreams in my life that were so realistic that I knew God was showing me something. However, the way I normally hear God is way more subtle.

Usually I will sense within myself God directing me in one direction or another. I believe that is when His spirit is speaking to me. We must be careful and understand that God will never say something to us or direct us in a way that does not line up with His Word and His nature.

Sometimes when I am asking for direction He answers by allowing a certain door of opportunity to open or close. Many times, when I have prayed for other people I have seen the thing I have prayed for happen.

My favorite way to hear God in our conversation is when I am listening, and a peace comes over me. This peace is described as the peace that passes all understanding. Philippians 4: 6-7 says.

"Do not be anxious about anything, but in every situation, by prayer and petition with thanksgiving, present your requests to God. And the peace of God, which transcends all understanding, will guard your hearts and minds in Christ Jesus".

I think the thing we struggle with most is that we have been so programmed to the idea that if we cannot see, hear, taste, touch, or smell something, it is not real. That is not true when it comes to God. God is spirit. As we grow in Him we begin to understand that there is a 6th sense which is spiritual. John 4:24 says.

"God is spirit, and His worshipers must worship Him in spirit and in truth."

Romans 8:26-27 says.

In the same way, the Spirit helps us in our weakness.

We do not know what we ought to pray for, but the Spirit himself intercedes for us through wordless groans. And he who searches our hearts knows the mind of the Spirit, because the Spirit intercedes for God's people in accordance with the will of God.

I have learned over 40 years of praying that God most often speaks to me in a quiet voice and to hear it I must be still. 1 Kings 19:9-13 tells this story of Elijah the prophet,

And the word of the LORD came to him: "What are you doing here, Elijah?" He replied, "I have been very zealous for the LORD God Almighty. The Israelites have rejected your covenant, torn down your altars, and put your prophets to death with the sword. I am the only one left, and now they are trying to kill me too." The LORD said, "Go out and stand on the mountain in the presence of the LORD, for the LORD is about to pass by." Then a great and powerful wind tore the mountains apart and shattered the rocks before the LORD, but the LORD was not in the wind. After the wind there was an earthquake, but the LORD was not in the earthquake. After the earthquake came a fire, but the LORD was not in the fire. And after the fire came a gentle whisper. When Elijah heard it, he pulled his cloak over his face and went out and stood at the mouth of the cave. Then a voice said to him, "What are you doing here, Elijah?"

Elijah knew the sound of that gentle whisper was God's voice. He realized that God does not reveal himself only in powerful, miraculous ways. To look for God only in something big such as a rally, a church conference, a highly visible leader, or a great miracle, may be to miss him because he is often found gently whispering in the quietness of a humbled heart. We must step back from the noise and activity of our busy lives and listen humbly and quietly for His guidance. Sometimes it comes when you least expect it.

When I think about prayer I am always amazed at how great men pray, especially the great men in the Bible. I have never worried about being eloquent when talking to God. However, I do try to think about what I am going to say and how I say it. I think that if we were meeting with the President of the United States or the king of a country, we would be careful about our choice of words, if for nothing else but to be respectful. Well when we pray to God we are not communicating with a president or a king of a country, we are talking to the King of the universe. The One whose Kingdom is greater than all Kingdom's. Let us look at how some of the great men of the Bible prayed.

In Deuteronomy 9:25-29 Moses laid prostrate before the Lord because the children of Israel had disobeyed. He prayed to the LORD and said,

"Sovereign LORD do not destroy your people, your own inheritance that you redeemed by your great power and brought out of Egypt with a mighty hand. Remember your servants Abraham, Isaac, and Jacob. Overlook the stubbornness of these people, their wickedness, and their sin. Otherwise, the country from which you brought us will say, 'Because the LORD was not able to take them into the land he had promised them, and because he hated them, he brought them out to put them to death in the wilderness.' But they are your people, your inheritance that you brought out by your great power and your outstretched arm."

In Nehemiah 1:5,11

Nehemiah was grieved that the Children of Israel had been captured and the walls of Jerusalem were destroyed. He prayed, "Lord, the God of heaven, the great and awesome God, who keeps his covenant of love with those who love him and keep his commandments, let your ear be attentive and your eyes open to hear the prayer your servant is praying before you day and night for your servants, the people of Israel. I confess the sins we Israelites, including myself and my father's family, have committed against you. We have acted very wickedly toward you. We have not obeyed the commands, decrees, and laws you gave your servant Moses. "Remember the instruction you gave your servant Moses, saying, 'If you are unfaithful, I will scatter you among the *nations, but if you return to me and obey my commands, then even if your exiled people are at the farthest horizon, I will gather them from there and bring them to the place I have chosen as a dwelling for my Name.' "They are your servants and your people, whom you redeemed by your great strength and your mighty hand. Lord, let your ear be attentive to the prayer of this your servant and to the prayer of your servants who delight in revering your name. Give your servant success today by granting him favor in the presence of this man."*

Daniel the great prophet cried out to God for himself and the people.   Daniel 9:3-19,

"Lord, the great and awesome God, who keeps his covenant of love with those who love him and keep his commandments, we have sinned and done wrong. We have been wicked and have rebelled; we have turned away from your commands and laws. We have not listened to your servants, the prophets, who spoke in your name to our kings, our princes, and our ancestors, and to all the people of the land. Lord, you are righteous, but this day we are covered with shame—the people of Judah and the inhabitants of Jerusalem and all Israel, both near and far, in all the countries where you have scattered us because of our unfaithfulness to you. We and our kings, our princes and our ancestors are covered with shame, Lord, because we have sinned against you The Lord our God is merciful and forgiving, even though we have rebelled against him; we have not obeyed the

Lord our God or kept the laws he gave us through his servants the prophets. All Israel has transgressed your law and turned away, refusing to obey you. Therefore, the curses and sworn judgments written in the Law of Moses, the servant of God, have been poured out on us, because we have sinned against you. You have fulfilled the words spoken against us and against our rulers by bringing on us great disaster. Under the whole heaven nothing has ever been done like what has been done to Jerusalem. Just as it is written in the Law of Moses, all this disaster has come on us, yet we have not sought the favor of the Lord our God by turning from our sins and giving attention to your truth The Lord did not hesitate to bring the disaster on us, for the Lord our God is righteous in everything he does; yet we have not obeyed him. Now, Lord our God, who brought your people out of Egypt with a mighty hand and who made for yourself a name that endures to this day, we have sinned, we have done wrong. Lord, in keeping with all your righteous acts, turn away your anger and your wrath from Jerusalem, your city, your holy hill. Our sins and the iniquities of our ancestors have made Jerusalem and your people an object of scorn to all those around us. Now, our God, hear the prayers and petitions of your servant. For your sake, Lord, look with favor on your desolate sanctuary. Give ear, our God, and hear; open your eyes and see the desolation of the city that bears your Name. We do not make requests of you because we are righteous, but because of your great mercy. Lord, listen! Lord, forgive! Lord, hear and act! For your sake, my God, do not delay, because your city and your people bear your Name."

One of my favorite prayers in all the Bible is when the Apostle Paul prayed in Ephesian 3:14-21.

For this reason, I kneel before the Father, from whom every family in heaven and on earth derives its name. I pray that out of his glorious riches he may strengthen you with power through his Spirit in your inner being, so that Christ may dwell in your hearts through faith. And I pray that you, being rooted and established in love, may have power, together with all the Lord's holy people, to grasp how wide and long and high and deep is the love of Christ, and to know this love that surpasses knowledge—that you may be filled to the measure of all the fullness of God. Now to him who is able to do immeasurably more than all we ask or imagine, according to his power that is at work within us, to him be glory in the church and in Christ Jesus throughout all generations, for ever and ever! Amen.

Listen to these prayers from some of the great people of God in our times,

Martin Luther King Jr.
(1929–1968)

O God,…we thank Thee for Thy Church, founded upon Thy Word, that challenges us to do

more than sing and pray, but go out and work as though the very answer to our prayers depended on us and not upon Thee... Help us to realize that man was created to shine like the stars and live on through all eternity. Keep us, we pray, in perfect peace, help us to walk together, pray together, sing together, and live together until that day when all God's children, Black, White, Red, and Yellow, will rejoice in one common band of humanity in the kingdom of our Lord and of our God, we pray. Amen.

Elisabeth Elliot
(1926–2015)

Loving Lord and heavenly Father, I offer up today all that I am, all that I have, all that I do, and all that I suffer, to be Yours today and Yours forever. Give me grace, Lord, to do all that I know of Your holy will. Purify my heart, sanctify my thinking, correct my desires. Teach me, in all of today's work and trouble and joy, to respond with honest praise, simple trust, and instant obedience, that my life may be in truth a living sacrifice, by the power of Your Holy Spirit and in the name of Your Son Jesus Christ, my Master and my all. Amen.

The great evangelist Billy Graham and his famous Prayer for the Nation:
(1918-2018)

"Our Father and Our God, we praise You for Your goodness to our nation, giving us blessings far beyond what we deserve. Yet we know all is not right with America. We deeply need a moral and spiritual renewal to help us meet the many problems we face. Convict us of sin. Help us to turn to You in repentance and faith. Set our feet on the path of Your righteousness and peace. We pray today for our nation's leaders. Give them the wisdom to know what is right, and the courage to do it. You have said, "Blessed is the nation whose God is the Lord." May this be a new era for America, as we humble ourselves and acknowledge You alone as our Savior and Lord. This we pray in Your holy name, Amen."

There are many kinds of prayer. I want to share with you the ones that I have made a part of my life.

I start with individual praying. This would include the Lord's prayer and praying throughout the day as we have discussed. I do morning prayers (which include praying my prayer journal), bedtime prayers, praying a blessing over our meals, and communion prayers.

We will also discuss corporate praying when you are asked to pray out loud in a group such as offering a blessing at a meal with family or friends.

Being asked to pray at a meeting. Praying for someone who is sick, hurting, or going through a rough time. Being part of a prayer group that meets to pray together.

Morning prayers

Over the years I have made a habit to start my day with prayer. Most times it is with a cup of coffee and follows my scripture reading and memory verse practice. My morning prayers begin with the Lord's prayer followed by my prayer journal.

I need to say here that I am one that prays in my mind when I am alone. Some people like to pray out loud and that is fine. From time to time I will say some things out loud to the Lord especially when I am excited. I do not mean taking the Lord's name in vain which a Christ follower should try to avoid under all circumstances. But like if I make a good golf shot or catch a nice fish I will often say out loud "thank you Jesus."

I do not like to miss my morning prayers because it seems like my day never goes as well. However, if I do have to miss I always try to get it in throughout the day.

What is a prayer Journal?

I found that as the list of things I was praying for continued to get larger I needed to start writing it all down so I would not forget any.

I found that if I organized my thoughts it was easier. Over the years my journal has changed because of losing family members or friends who passed on. I am sure that people who journal this way organize it differently, so I would not say there is a right or wrong way. I always kept mine in the back of my bible, but in the last few years I have kept it on my laptop and smartphone. Over the years of praying my journal I have memorized it. This makes it nice when I am in a situation that doesn't allow me to read it, for instance if I'm lying in bed at night talking to the Lord, or if I'm driving down the road. I love doing it while I am walking in the mornings.

The best way I can help you see an example of a prayer journal is to share my own with you. I will be leaving some names blank so as not to embarrass anyone.

My prayer journal.

Recite the Lord's Prayer

Things I am thankful for

Your Word
Salvation
Forgiveness
Answered prayers
My health
My family
My friends

My home
The food I eat
The clothes I wear
The car and truck, Golf cart & clubs, Fishing boat and gear, Mower, and tools
Our finances

Prayers for Myself

Help me not be anxious or worried
Help me have a smile of my face, song in my heart
Help me to live as though I am dying
Help me have a clear vision of mission and stay focused on it
Help me to try to be straightforward and honest
Help me not be jealous but be thankful for all I have
Help me not tear anyone down or build myself up
Help me understand giving and service
Help with my Church life
Help me not to be judgmental but let You do the judging
Help me to offer the grace and mercy to others that You gave me so freely
Help me recognize and minister to the needs of others
To be quick to listen, slow to speak, slow to anger
To be patient kind and warmhearted
Fill me with your Holy Spirit so I know what to say and not to say and know what to do and not to do
More of you Lord and less of me, you must increase I must decrease

Help me be a good witness and a blessing to
someone today
Fill me with wisdom and knowledge so I might see the
deep and hidden things
Help me know where my faith and your will intersect
Help me to understand my gifts
Help me to understand prophecy
Help me see heaven
Help me have a pure heart
Help me have a strong mind thru faith
Help me to make the cross my central focus

Prayers for my family

Bless Debbie, James, Jenny, Nate, Kimmy
Bless Adam, Taylor, Levi
Bless Kyle, Jenn, and the girls
Bless Tony, Judy, and the boys
Bless Delano, Lauren, Carmen

Prayers for my Friends

Bless these friends,
E... and family
S... and family
M... and family
B... and family
L... and family
C... and family
G... and family

S... and M...
O... and E...
E... and D...
D... and family
A... and family
D... and family
E.. and N...
T... and S...
R... and D...
R..., D..., K... and R...
The W... family and granddaughter S...
C...
J...
H... and R...
P... and J...
R.M. and family
J.. and family
J... and M...
Frank C...
Mary E...
C... and J...
L... and J...
B..., A... and G...
E... and T...
Johnny E...
Philip B...
John L...
Florida friends
Dave S...
Eddie M...
N..., S..., and brother B...

Jimmy H... and family
K... and Pam...

Prayers for my Country, leaders, and Soldiers

Help me to know how to pray for our country and
leaders
Thank you for our freedom
Be with our soldiers especially those in harm's way
Be with our policemen, firefighters, teachers

Prayers for our finances

Bless B properties...R and M
Protect our liquid assets
Bless C... bank
Bless S... funds
Bless V...funds
Bless S...funds

Prayers for our Ministries

Bless CCA.....D... and family, J... and R..., M... and
P..., J..., W..., Mrs. D, B... R..., Mrs. J, the staff,
students & finances
Bless Wayside.....T... and N...
Bless Youth for Christ......K... and D...
Bless Go International......L... and J...
Bless D... and M...
Bless B... and J...their ministry and granddaughter K...

Bless Southeast Christian Church K... and family,
D...and family, R and family, M...and family, campus
pastors
Bless Christ Fellowship church and staff
Bless Shelby Christian and staff
Bless Henry Christian and staff
Bless Awake ministries and staff
Bless Serenity Center and crew
Bless Celebrate Recovery...J... and T...
Bible Baptist church.....B..., R..., N..., K...
Billy Graham ministries, Samaritan Purse, and
Franklin Graham

I pray all of this in the name of Jesus, Amen.

Bedtime prayers

Bedtime prayers for me are shorter than
morning prayers. I usually say them laying in the bed
just before I go to sleep. Some people kneel by their
bed as they were taught as children. I think that is
great. There are times when I will do that especially if
I am struggling with something. I think as we age it
gets harder to kneel for very long. It is funny how I
always start with a simple children's prayer that I
suspect you have heard before. It goes like this.
Now I lay me down to sleep,
I pray thee Lord my soul to keep.
If I should die before I wake,
I pray thee lord my soul to take.

I then follow that by praying for my immediate family by name and then for any of my friends that are really going through a difficult time. I thank the Lord for a good day and ask for a good night's sleep.

I have friends who pray together as couples at night. I think that is wonderful.

My wife and I pray together for our meals regularly. Sometimes when we, our family, or one of our friends are going through a difficult time we will pray together about that.

Mealtime prayers

Over the years I discovered how important it was to give thanks to God for the food we eat.

This prayer is often referred to as grace. A grace is typically a short prayer said before eating. Some traditions hold that grace and thanksgiving imparts a blessing which sanctifies the meal.

Sometimes this prayer is called the blessing. We bless God when thanking Him for our food. Paul wrote in Colossians 3,17,

"Whatever you do in word or deed, do everything in the name of the Lord Jesus, giving thanks to God the Father through Him."

My family and I always pray at meals. We share in who says the prayer. We usually thank God for the food we are about to eat. Sometimes we thank Him for the hands that have prepared the food. We also will ask for blessings on our family and friends, especially if there is someone ill or going through a hard time.

Sometimes we are praying over a special meal such as Thanksgiving or Christmas. At those times we will gather in a circle and hold hands. At the Thanksgiving meal we will sometimes go around the circle and have each person tell one thing they are thankful for. At the Christmas meal we will always give thanks for the birth of Jesus and what He has done for us.

I have always loved the prayer that many of my Catholic friends pray at mealtime. It goes like this.

"Bless us, O Lord, and these Thy gifts, which we are about to receive from Thy bounty. Through Christ, our Lord. Amen."

Usually the one who says this prayer makes the sign of the cross on their chest as they say, *"in the name of the Father, Son and Holy Spirit."* I just find this prayer to be so comforting and holy.

Oftentimes when I am saying grace, I will ask God to bless those less fortunate and that do not have food to eat.

One thing I have seen become uncomfortable is when you are sharing a meal with someone and you are not sure of where they stand when it comes to religion or how they feel about public prayer. I would not want to embarrass anyone. I usually will try my best to sense the direction the Holy Spirit is leading me. Most often I will simply ask them if they mind me offering a blessing. I can never remember anyone being offended or objecting. But the truth is that you can always bow your head and have a silent prayer. I guess there could be a fine line between us not wanting to offend someone and us not being ashamed of our faith.

When it comes right down to it, a situation like this could present an opportunity for us to witness our faith. As we grow in our faith we begin to look for those opportunities. You never really know what is going on inside of people. It could be they have been struggling and looking for some answers. Your witness by giving thanks for the meal and the fellowship you are having with them, might be the catapult they needed to do some investigating.

Communion prayers

When we begin attending church we learn that one part of the church service is communion. I attend an independent Christian church and the tradition is to partake in communion each week. Some churches do communion monthly or quarterly. Communion is considered a sacrament.

You see Jesus introduce communion during the last meal He had with His disciples before He was Crucified. He wanted them to have a way to remember Him and what He had done for them. He gave them bread to represent His body that would be broken and wine that would represent His blood that would be shed for all of humanity. This is all recorded in Matthew 26: 26-30,

"While they were eating, Jesus took bread, and when he had given thanks, he broke it and gave it to his disciples, saying, "Take and eat; this is my body." Then he took a cup, and when he had given thanks, he gave it to them, saying, "Drink from it, all of you. This is my blood of the covenant, which is poured out for many for the forgiveness of sins. I tell you; I will not drink from this fruit of the vine from now on until that day when I drink it new with you in my Father's kingdom." When they had sung a hymn, they went out to the Mount of Olives.

Usually before we eat the bread or cracker that represents Jesus body, and drink the juice or wine that represents His blood, we are given time to meditate (pray). During this time of meditation, I like to reflect on any ill feelings I might have toward anyone and ask God to forgive me and help me get those feelings in line with His love. I also will examine myself to ascertain if there is any unconfessed sin in me and ask God for His forgiveness.

We read the words of Paul in 1st Corinthians 11:23-29.

"For I received from the Lord what I also passed on to you. The Lord Jesus, on the night he was betrayed, took bread, and when he had given thanks, he broke it and said, "This is my body, which is for you; do this in remembrance of me." In the same way, after supper he took the cup, saying, "This cup is the new covenant in my blood; do this, whenever you drink it, in remembrance of me." For whenever you eat this bread and drink this cup, you proclaim the Lord's death until he comes.

So then, whoever eats the bread or drinks the cup of the Lord in an unworthy manner will be guilty of sinning against the body and blood of the Lord. Everyone ought to examine themselves before they eat of the bread and drink from the cup. For those who eat and drink without discerning the body of Christ eat and drink judgment on themselves.

After the elements are served there is usually a communion song and a time to pray. It is during this time that I thank God for giving His son for us. I thank Jesus for what He had to go through and tell Him I am sorry that He had to endure that for my sake.

Corporate Praying

When I talk about corporate prayer I am referring to praying out loud in front of others. It could be just as simple as sharing prayer with a friend or group of friends where each person prays, as they are led, for certain needs or issues.

As you grow in the faith you may find yourself in the position of praying for someone who is in need. They could be ill or going through a tragedy or any number of things in their life.

You may be asked someday to pray for and in front of a gathering of people. It could be in church or Sunday school, in a meeting or event, or to offer a blessing for a meal with family or friends.

I am asked to say these prayers quite often. In the beginning I felt a little uneasy and I think that is natural. Some of us are just uncomfortable speaking in front of others. Over time I have become more accustomed to doing it. I would like to offer some suggestions that may help you and the folks that you are praying for.

First be sensitive to the leading of the Holy Spirit. The following are verses that are close to the context in which I am speaking.

Luke 12: 11-12

"When you are brought before synagogues, rulers and authorities, do not worry about how you will defend yourselves or what you will say, for the Holy Spirit will teach you at that time what you should say."

Romans 8: 26

"In the same way, the Spirit helps us in our weakness. We do not know what we ought to pray for, but the Spirit himself intercedes for us through wordless groans. And he who searches our hearts knows the mind of the Spirit, because the Spirit intercedes for God's people in accordance with the will of God."

2nd Corinthians 2:13

"This is what we speak, not in words taught us by human wisdom but in words taught by the Spirit, explaining spiritual realities with Spirit-taught words."

I believe that in the same way the Holy Spirit helps in the context of these scriptures, He can help us know what to say, even when praying.

I try during these times of prayer to choose my words with care. I realize that I am not only talking to God, but I am being used by God at the same time. Sometimes when I am praying to God alone I will catch myself saying, " I shouldn't have said or asked that the way I did". It is not that easy to unsay something when you are praying out loud with others. So, I find myself trying to allow the Holy Spirit to lead me and at the same time being careful with my words. I have found there is nothing wrong with taking your time when talking to God.

In Chapter 4 we are going to be discussing in detail another thing that helps us at these times. It is knowing scripture and having it memorized. Often when I am praying for or in front of others, a scripture will come to my mind and I will speak it. I believe the Holy Spirit reminds me of the scripture at that time. It will always be a scripture that speaks to the need I am talking to God about. I always want to be careful that I am not trying to make an impression on people that I am a super Christian or that I am showing off. It is usually something that comes naturally.

When I pray I speak to God. When I read the bible God speaks to me.

When I pray scripture I pray the words of God. Prayer and God's word are inseparably linked together.

Lastly, there are certain special times when I have been asked to pray at a large gathering. It is not uncommon for me to think about and know what I am going to pray ahead of time. I have even written out prayers ahead of time, especially when I feel that I might be nervous for whatever reason.

Even though there are some people of faith that might be critical of this, I think it is fine. I see great men in the Bible, even Jesus, whose prayers were recorded for us to read. I have seen great people of modern times write out their prayers. I mentioned a few of them earlier in this chapter that I really admired.

One word of caution! I have seen people use corporate prayer as a platform to push their agenda. Oftentimes it is a political statement. An example would be something like this, "Lord help us all to know that you want such and such to happen or so and so to win." I always feel let down when I hear something like that, and I am not sure that God appreciates it.

One final thought, "I have found the more I talk to God, the easier it is to talk to God!"

Praying in unknown Languages

There is another kind of prayer that I am going to mention here. I will not spend much time on it because it is not a prayer that I do. I am referring to praying in unknown languages (speaking in tongues).

Most Christ followers will be confronted with this praying at some point. If your family or friends are Pentecostal you will be introduced to it early on. If you do not follow the Pentecostal tradition you may never encounter it. When I became a Christ follower in the mid 1970's there was a movement referred to as the charismatic movement. Some of my friends talked to me about it and I tried to go that direction, but honestly, I never felt that I fit in.

Several of my best lifetime friends are Pentecostal and it has not affected our friendship or love for each other in any way. We do great working beside each other in different ministries.

I have not found in scripture of Jesus speaking in tongues or of Him teaching about speaking in tongues. The first time I read of tongues is in the book of Acts. It happened on the day of Pentecost. People were speaking in languages that they were not familiar with and people who knew that language were understanding them. The Apostle Paul speaks of tongues a lot in the book of 1st Corinthians. After much study I cannot conclude he teaches that everyone is given that gift. He does teach that it is one of several gifts the Holy Spirit gives us.

I have close friends in main line denomination churches as well as friends in Independent Christian churches that do not believe that tongues or prophecy exist today. On the other hand, I have close friends in Pentecostal and Holiness churches that believe that tongues and prophecy do exist. In fact, some of them believe if you do not have the gift of tongues you do not have the Holy Spirit the way they do.

I have never felt qualified to argue with either side. I must leave that up to God.

I can say that I am sure that God's spirit is in me and I do not appear to have the gift of tongues. I knew God's spirit came into me when I got saved because of the changes that happened and continue to happen in me. Also, because the Bible says God's spirit would come into me. I go back to what Peter said in the 2nd chapter of Acts.

'Repent and be baptized in the name of Jesus Christ, for the remission of your sins, and you will receive the gift of the Holy Spirit."

I have always felt that the evidence of the Holy Spirit in me has manifested itself in several ways and I pray that you are experiencing these same changes.

I have a stronger sense of right and wrong.

I no longer want to do the bad things I used to do.

I feel remorse now when I sin, that I never felt before.

I have a deep interest in scripture now that I never had before, and I can understand it more clearly each day.

I began to have the desire to attend church.

I am deeply touched in worship, preaching, and communion.

I want to help others, love them, and offer them grace and mercy, like I never did before.

I often experience a peace that I cannot explain. It is a peace that passes my understanding.

I developed a strong sense of urgency to do all the disciplines I describe here in this book.

I will leave this type of prayer to the preference of the reader. You can investigate and decide on your own. I would simply suggest that you continue to present yourself to God as a clean vessel, a living sacrifice, and ask Him to give you everything He wants you to have.

Romans 12: 1-2.

"Therefore, I urge you, brothers, and sisters, in view of God's mercy, to offer your bodies as a living sacrifice, holy and pleasing to God—this is your true and proper worship. Do not conform to the pattern of this world but be transformed by the renewing of your mind. Then you will be able to test and approve what God's will is—his good, pleasing and perfect will."

I would like to close this chapter with a story that was told to me recently. I think it is an example of how a simple conversation with God can change your life forever.

I have a friend whose name is Eddie Mason. Eddie is well known and respected in the town I live in, Shelbyville, Ky. Eddie was the Shelby County High School head basketball coach for many years. He was loved by all the kids who played for him as well as their parents. Eddie is now 80 years old and suffers from the same disease that caused me to have a double lung transplant (pulmonary fibrosis). He is homebound now on full time oxygen.

I enjoy spending time with Eddie and hearing stories of his life.

One recent afternoon I grabbed a couple of fish dinners from his favorite place along with his favorite drink Dr. Pepper. As we were eating together at his dining room table he shared this story and gave me permission to use it when I asked.

He said, "On March 10th of 1990 his team was playing Oldham Co. in the final game of the regionals." His son Greg was a senior and was all-state. Greg is now the head basketball coach at Center College in Danville, Ky. They had trailed by 4-6 points the whole game. Greg had only scored 6 points. The time had stopped, and Eddie said, "I looked up at the clock and there was 2 minutes 30 seconds left and we were down 6 points." I thought at this point Eddie was going to share with me some elaborate play he called that won the game. To my surprise he said, "I looked down at the floor and said, Lord I haven't asked you for much, but if you would let these boys win this game, I will never touch a drop of alcohol the rest of my life." Now Eddie was never a big drinker, maybe just a beer from time to time on Saturday.

He said that in the next 2 minutes Greg scored 12 points and they won the game. Eddie said, "that was 40 years ago, and I have never had a drop of alcohol since that night!"

I always want to keep in mind that the coach on the other side may have been praying the exact same prayer. Is that wrong? So how does God answer both prayers? To tell the truth I am not sure. I go back to the reality that prayer is a conversation with God. I must believe that even when we do not pray the most perfect prayer, He is still glad to hear from us.

I have found that some people do not believe that God answers prayers like that. I wish I could tell you the number of prayers I have prayed like that. Like I said earlier in this chapter sometimes God says yes, sometimes no, and sometimes not yet. So many times, he has said yes to me. There is one thing for sure, if we do not ask we will never know what God will do.

James 4:2-3.

" You do not have because you do not ask God. When you ask, you do not receive, because you ask with wrong motives, that you may spend what you get on your pleasures."

Mathew 7: 7-11.

"Ask and it will be given to you; seek and you will find; knock and the door will be opened to you. For everyone who asks receives; the one who seeks finds; and to the one who knocks, the door will be opened. "Which of you, if your son asks for bread, will give him a stone?

Or if he asks for a fish, will give him a snake? If you, then, though you are evil, know how to give good gifts to your children, how much more will your Father in heaven give good gifts to those who ask him!"

1st John 5: 13-15.

"I write these things to you who believe in the name of the Son of God so that you may know that you have eternal life. This is the confidence we have in approaching God: that if we ask anything according to his will, he hears us. And if we know that he hears us—whatever we ask—we know that we have what we asked of him."

To sum it up.

When I am praying, communicating with God, I am not always asking for something. Sometimes I am confessing, sometimes I am thanking Him for things, sometimes I am pouring my heart out to Him, sometimes I am just needing someone to talk to. Whatever the case I am always hoping to be in His will. I do not always know what His will is. But I am willing to accept His will and whatever He has for me. I know He is a loving Father, and He wants what is best for me.

As I have accepted these things in faith He has continued to be faithful to me.

I believe the more we give of ourselves to God, the more He gives Himself to us.

Chapter 3
Scripture Reading

I believe that for the Christ Follower the Bible is our road map. I have heard it said that the Bible is a love letter from God.

In the Old Testament Joshua 1:8 says.

"Keep this Book of the Law always on your lips; meditate on it day and night, so that you may be careful to do everything written in it. Then you will be prosperous and successful."

In the New Testament 2nd Timothy 3:16-17 says.

"All Scripture is God-breathed and is useful for teaching, rebuking, correcting and training in righteousness, so that the servant of God may be thoroughly equipped for every good work."

I mentioned earlier that prayer may be the most important discipline, however I think scripture reading is right there with it. When we are praying we are having a conversation with God and when we are reading scripture we are learning who God is.

I began reading the Bible 40 years ago after being saved at the age of 27. After I got saved I borrowed a Bible from my wife. If I remember correctly it was a King James Version. I started at the beginning and read it to the end in a year.

I fell in love with reading the Bible. I decided to read it again the next year. I found a reading plan that gives you Old Testament and New Testament verses each day. This is referred to as a lectionary. This became a pattern for me and now I have done it forty times.

The first Bible of my own was a New King James Version. About 15 years later I switched to the New International Version. Over the years I would try a new Bible each year that would have commentary in it. I eventually settled into my favorite Bible which is the New International Version Life Application Bible.

I want to spend some time talking a little bit about the makeup of the Bible and the different translations.

First, the Bible is not one book. It is a collection of 66 books that are divided into two sections called the Old testament (OT) and the New Testament (NT). There are 39 books in the OT and 27 books in the NT.

I always try to advise folks, that are new to the faith, that they should try to read all the way through the Bible at least once. You get to see God's plan all the way from creation to the end of times. In the OT you learn about God the Father and in the NT you learn about God the Son (Jesus). In both the OT and the NT, you learn about God the (Holy Spirit).

After I read the OT, the NT made more sense to me. It is like all the way through the OT you are building up to what is going to happen in the NT. The prophetic passages in the OT tell us about the coming of Jesus, while the gospel passages of the NT teach us about Jesus.

The following is an overview of the Bible including each of the books, the author, the date it was written, and a description of the book. Keep in mind that though I list an author for each book, the truth is that it all was written (inspired) by the Holy Spirit.

2nd Peter 1:21 says.

"For prophecy never had its origin in the human will, but prophets, though human, spoke from God as they were carried along by the Holy Spirit."

Old Testament

A collection of divinely inspired books written between 1450 B.C. and 430 B.C., the Old Testament is a historical record of God's people, laws, sayings and promises that function as a model for moral living and conduct.

1. Genesis
Moses
1450-1410 B.C.
Meaning "the beginning or origin of something", Genesis is the first book of the Bible, recording Creation, the fall of man and the early years of the nation of Israel.

2. Exodus
Moses
1450-1410 B.C

God appoints Moses to lead the Israelites out of slavery in Egypt to the Promised Land of Canaan, establishing a special relationship with them on the way to Mount Sinai.

3. Leviticus
Moses
1445-1444 B.C.

God gives Israel rules to live by and instructions to present themselves holy before Him.

4. Numbers
Moses
1450-1410 B.C.

A sequel to Exodus, Numbers takes its name from two censuses (or "numberings") of the people of Israel, following their journey through the wilderness for forty years.

5. Deuteronomy
Moses 1407-1406 B.C.

A farewell speech from Moses to the people of Israel shortly before his death, Deuteronomy recaps the promises of God and provides instructions to obey Him in the Promised Land.

6. Joshua
Joshua & possibly Phinehas
1405-1383 B.C.

A book of conquest, Joshua details the Israelites' invasion and eventual occupation of the Promised Land through faith and action.

7. Judges
Probably Samuel
1086-1004 B.C.
Israel enters a cycle of sin, suffering defeat and oppression, only to cry out to God for deliverance, who sends leaders (called "judges") to help them.

8. Ruth
Unknown
1375-1050 B.C.
Occurring during some of the darkest days in Israel's history, Ruth follows the journey of two widows who lose everything but find hope through God.

9. 1st Samuel
Samuel, Nathan & Gad
930 B.C.
Israel rejects God's chosen leader, Samuel (a judge), and demands a king despite God's warnings.

10. 2nd Samuel
Unknown
930 B.C.
The life and career of King David, who subdues Israel's enemies and doubles the size of the kingdom but is not without failings.

11. 1st Kings
Unknown
560-538 B.C.
Israel enjoys a period of peace and prosperity under King Solomon, but later splits in two after Rehoboam (his son) takes the throne.

12. 2nd Kings
Unknown
560-538 B.C.
The kings of Israel and Judah ignore God and His prophets, eventually falling captive to invading nations and are exiled to foreign lands.

13. 1st Chronicles
Ezra
430 B.C.
Written to encourage the people returning from Babylonian exile, 1 Chronicles recaps the history and genealogy of Israel, emphasizing the spiritual significance of David and future Messianic King.

14. 2nd Chronicles
Ezra
430 B.C.
A continuation of the previous book, 2 Chronicles focuses on the kings of Israel, from King Solomon and the building of the temple, to subsequent division, exile and return from captivity.

15. Ezra
Ezra
450 B.C.
Fulfilling the promises of God, the Israelites return from exile after seventy years and rebuild the temple.

16. Nehemiah
Nehemiah
445-432 B.C.
Despite local opposition, Nehemiah returns to Jerusalem from exile, rallying the people to rebuild the city walls and gates in just fifty-two days.

17. Esther
Unknown
483-471 B.C.
Occurring during the exile of Israel, Esther is a Jewish queen to a Persian king, who intercedes on behalf of her people to save them from a genocidal plot.

18. Job
Possibly Job
2100-1800 B.C.
A righteous man named Job loses everything and suffers greatly but remains faithful to God and is blessed abundantly.

19. Psalms
David, Asaph, the sons of Korah, Solomon, Heman, Ethan & Moses
1440-586 B.C.
A collection of 150 songs of worship and praise to God that includes prophecies of the coming Messiah.

20. Proverbs
Solomon, Agur & Lemuel
970-930 B.C.
The book of Proverbs contains God's divine wisdom, covering a variety of topics for every area of life.

21. Ecclesiastes
Solomon
935 B.C.
Solomon's analysis of life: it is it which is meaningless and empty without God.

22. Song of Songs
Solomon
970-930 B.C.
A passionate yet gentle song of love between a husband and wife, symbolizing God's relationship with us.

23. Isaiah
Isaiah
700-681 B.C.
The first book of the Major Prophets, Isaiah contains warnings of God's coming judgement and detailed prophecies about the Messiah.

24. Jeremiah
Jeremiah
627-586 B.C.
Known as the weeping prophet, Jeremiah passionately pleads with the people to repent before the coming Babylonian captivity, but is ignored.

25. Lamentations
Jeremiah
586 B.C.
Lamentations is a book of sadness that reflects on the destruction of Jerusalem and captivity of Israel.

26. Ezekiel
Ezekiel
571 B.C.
Ezekiel is called by God to preach a message of judgement and deliverance for the captives living in Babylon.

27. Daniel
Daniel
535 B.C.
Like Ezekiel, Daniel has been taken to Babylon in captivity and receives prophetic visions while serving in the courts of the king.

28. Hosea
Hosea
715 B.C.
The first book of the Minor Prophets, Hosea is a tragic love story that demonstrates God's unending love for His people despite their unfaithfulness.

29. Joel
Joel
835-796 B.C.
Joel warns the people to repent and turn back to God before judgement falls upon them.

30. Amos
Amos
760-750 B.C.
A shepherd named Amos prophesies to the northern kingdom which has become self-sufficient and indifferent towards God during a time of great prosperity.

31. Obadiah
Obadiah
627-586 B.C.

Only one chapter, Obadiah demonstrates God's ongoing protection of His people and coming judgement on the nation of Edom, which was indifferent during the Babylonian plunder of Jerusalem.

32. Jonah
Jonah
785-760 B.C.

A reluctant prophet, Jonah is sent by God to Nineveh, but refuses and learns the futility of it in the belly of a giant fish.

33. Micah
Micah
742-687 B.C.

Micah warns of the coming judgement that will eventually exile the nation and includes some of the clearest predictions of the Messiah.

34. Nahum
Nahum
663-654 B.C.

Nahum is the second prophet sent to Nineveh (Jonah being the first) to preach God's judgement on the Assyrian city and empire.

35. Habakkuk
Habakkuk
612-589 B.C.

God answers Habakkuk's complaints of wickedness and injustice in the land.

36. Zephaniah
Zephaniah
640-621 B.C.
Written shortly before the fall of Judah (Southern Kingdom of Israel) to Babylonian conquest, Zephaniah warns the people and the surrounding nations that the day of the Lord is near.

37. Haggai
Haggai
520 B.C.
Written after the Babylonian exile, work to rebuild the temple in Jerusalem had halted due to opposition and spiritual apathy, so Haggai motivates the people to finish.

38. Zechariah
Zechariah
520-480 B.C.
Zechariah ministered with Haggai after the 70-year exile, encouraging the remnant to return to God.

39. Malachi
Malachi
430 B.C.
The last book of the Old Testament, Malachi is a beautiful expression of God's love for a nation that continues to disobey Him.

New Testament

The New Testament is a collection of twenty-seven sacred books that center on the life, death, resurrection, and teachings of Jesus Christ.

40. Matthew
Matthew (Levi)
A.D. 60-65
The first book of the New Testament, the Gospel of Matthew was primarily written for the Jews and references many Old Testament prophecies that were fulfilled by Jesus.

41. Mark
John Mark
A.D. 55-65
Mark is the shortest Gospel, which emphasizes Jesus' servanthood and miracles.

42. Luke
Luke
A.D. 60
Unlike the other Gospel writers, Luke was a Gentile who wrote an account of Jesus' life for those outside the Jewish faith.

43. John
John
A.D. 85-90
The last of the four Gospels, John is an eyewitness account of Jesus' ministry that focuses on the deeper meaning of events surrounding Christ's life, death, and resurrection.

44. Acts
Luke
A.D. 63-70
A historical narrative of the early church which was empowered by the Holy Spirit to spread the Good News.

45. Romans
Paul
A.D. 70
An epistle to the believers in Rome (hence the name) where Paul plans to visit, Romans sets a theological foundation for faith through Jesus.

46. 1st Corinthians
Paul
A.D. 55
The first of two letters from Paul to the believers in Corinth, 1 Corinthians was written in response to divisions and problems facing the local church.

47. 2nd Corinthians
Paul
A.D. 55-57
The second and final letter from Paul to the church in Corinth, 2 Corinthians deals with persisting problems facing the believers there and warns against false teachers.

48. Galatians
Paul
A.D. 49
A letter from Paul to the church in Galatia, the book is a foundational study that addresses the problem of Jewish legalism and the fullness of salvation found in Jesus.

49. Ephesians
Paul
A.D. 60
Written to the church in Ephesus during Paul's first imprisonment, Ephesians covers a variety of subjects including the gift of grace, love and how to walk as fruitful followers of Jesus.

50. Philippians
Paul
A.D. 61
An encouraging letter from Paul to the church in Philippi explaining the attitude and outlook believers must have to experience the joy of the Lord.

51. Colossians
Paul
A.D. 60
In this letter, Paul refutes certain false teachings that are impeding the church in Colossae, reaffirming the deity and superiority of Jesus Christ.

52. 1st Thessalonians
Paul
A.D. 51
The first of two letters to the believers in
Thessalonica, Paul writes to encourage and
strengthen the church, emphasizing the principles of
holy living through faith, hope and love.

53. 2nd Thessalonians
Paul
A.D. 51
A follow-up letter of encouragement to the persecuted
church of Thessalonica, Paul reaffirms Jesus' second
coming and matters preceding that event.

54. 1st Timothy
Paul
A.D. 54
A letter from Paul to a young pastor named Timothy,
offering guidance and important principles for church
leadership that still apply today.

55. 2nd Timothy
Paul
A.D. 67
The second of two letters to Timothy, are probably
Paul's final chronological epistle, urging his protégé to
remain strong and faithful to Jesus.

56. Titus
Paul
A.D. 65
A letter of guidance from Paul to Titus to address challenges facing his leadership of the churches on the island of Crete.

57. Philemon
Paul
A.D. 60
Consisting of only one chapter, the book is a short but profound letter from Paul to Philemon requesting forgiveness for a runaway slave named Onesimus.

58. Hebrews
Unknown
A.D. 68
A letter urging Jewish believers not to return to their former traditions, summarizing key Biblical characters and events to emphasize the hope of salvation through Jesus.

59. James
James (Jesus' half-brother)
A.D. 49
A hard-hitting letter from James, encouraging believers to have a genuine faith with an emphasis on results.

60. 1st Peter
Peter
A.D. 65
The focus of Peter's first letter is persecution, sharing inspiring words of comfort for Christians living as an oppressed minority in the Roman Empire.

61. 2nd Peter
Peter
A.D. 66
Peter's second letter warns against false teachers and reaffirms important spiritual truths.

62. 1st John
John
A.D. 90-95
Written to oppose heretical doctrine, the first letter from John echoes the Gospel, encouraging Christians to love one another and keep Jesus' commands.

63. 2nd John
John
A.D. 90-95
A brief letter from John to "the chosen lady", urging believers to love one another and to be on guard against false teachings.

64. 3rd John
John
A.D. 90-95
The shortest book in the Bible, 3 John commends Gaius and Demetrius for their faithful service.

65. Jude
Jude (Jesus' half-brother)
A.D. 65
A letter from Jude to address false teachings and urge Christians to defend the truth of the Good News.

66. Revelation
John
A.D. 95
Written during John's imprisonment on the island of Patmos, Revelation is an apocalyptic book that contains prophetic visions of the Spiritual Realms and Jesus' return to Earth.

If you decide to read completely through the Bible I would recommend a reading plan. There are many different types of plans. You can choose a one-year plan or two-year plan etc. You can also decide to read it from start to finish or you could read passages from both the OT and the NT each day.

I have a Bible on the shelf I really enjoyed in the mid 1990's. It is called the One-year Bible. You start on January 1st. And it gives you an OT and NT reading along with a Psalm and Proverb each day until December 31st.

Many study Bibles you buy will have a reading plan in them. You can also go online and download an app to use.

The past 2 years I have done something new that I have really enjoyed. I downloaded an app called The Tecarta Bible app. It has a 365-day reading plan. You can pick the Bible you want, and I picked the New International Version Life Application Bible. I simply pick the day of the year and it gives me the daily reading with study notes. I have found I really like reading on the computer. It has been very handy for me because of having to spend so much time traveling for health issues. I have learned to take notes by copying and pasting to my memo pad. I also have it synced up to my smartphone. I have access to concordances at the same time. A concordance is a tool you can use to find something in the Bible by simply having a name or a topic.

On the following page you will see an image of a reading plan that is like the one I used +for many years.

Bible Bookmark - Daily Reading

January

Day	New Testament	Old Testament
1	Mt 1	Ge 1-2
2	Mt 2	Ge 3-5
3	Mt 3	Ge 6-7
4	Mt 4	Ge 8-10
5	Mt 5:1-20	Ge 11-12
6	Mt 5:21-48	Ge 13-15
7	Mt 6:1-15	Ge 16-18
8	Mt 6:16-34	Ge 19-20
9	Mt 7	Ge 21-22
10	Mt 8	Ge 23-24
11	Mt 9:1-17	Ge 25
12	Mt 9:18-38	Ge 26-27
13	Mt 10:1-15	Ge 28-29
14	Mt 10:16-42	Ge 30
15	Mt 11	Ge 31-32
16	Mt 12:1-8	Ge 33-34
17	Mt 12:9-32	Ge 35-36
18	Mt 12:33-50	Ge 37-38
19	Mt 13:1-23	Ge 39-40
20	Mt 13:24-46	Ge 41-42
21	Mt 13:47-58	Ge 43-44
22	Mt 14	Ge 45-46
23	Mt 15:1-20	Ge 47-48
24	Mt 15:21-39	Ge 49-50
25	Mt 16	Ex 1-3
26	Mt 17	Ex 4-5
27	Mt 18:1-14	Ex 6-7
28	Mt 18:15-35	Ex 8-9
29	Mt 19	Ex 10-12
30	Mt 20:1-16	Ex 13-14
31	Mt 20:17-34	Ex 15-16

February

Day	New Testament	Old Testament
1	Mt 21:1-27	Ex 17-19
2	Mt 21:28-46	Ex 20-21
3	Mt 22:1-22	Ex 22-23
4	Mt 22:23-46	Ex 24-25
5	Mt 23:1-22	Ex 26-27
6	Mt 23:23-39	Ex 28-29
7	Mt 24:1-28	Ex 30-31
8	Mt 24:29-51	Ex 32-33
9	Mt 25:1-13	Ex 34-35
10	Mt 25:14-46	Ex 36-37
11	Mt 26:1-13	Ex 38-39
12	Mt 26:14-35	Ex 40
13	Mt 26:36-56	Le 1-4
14	Mt 26:57-75	Le 5-6
15	Mt 27:1-26	Le 7-8
16	Mt 27:27-56	Le 9-10
17	Mt 27:57-66	Le 11-12
18	Mt 28	Le 13
19	Mk 1:1-28	Le 14-15
20	Mk 1:29-45	Le 16-17
21	Mk 2	Le 18-19
22	Mk 3:1-19	Le 20-22
23	Mk 3:20-35	Le 23
24	Mk 4:1-25	Le 24-25
25	Mk 4:26-41	Le 26
26	Mk 5:1-20	Le 27
27	Mk 5:21-43	Nu 1-2
28	Mk 6:1-29	Nu 3-4

March

Day	New Testament	Old Testament
1	Mk 6:30-56	Nu 5-6
2	Mk 7:1-23	Nu 7
3	Mk 7:24-37	Nu 8
4	Mk 8:1-21	Nu 9-10
5	Mk 8:22-38	Nu 11-13
6	Mk 9:1-29	Nu 14
7	Mk 9:30-50	Nu 15-16
8	Mk 10:1-31	Nu 17-18
9	Mk 10:32-52	Nu 19-20
10	Mk 11:1-14	Nu 21-22
11	Mk 11:15-33	Nu 23-24
12	Mk 12:1-27	Nu 25-26
13	Mk 12:28-44	Nu 27-28
14	Mk 13:1-23	Nu 29-30
15	Mk 13:24-37	Nu 31
16	Mk 14:1-21	Nu 32-33
17	Mk 14:22-52	Nu 34-35
18	Mk 14:53-72	Nu 36
19	Mk 15:1-20	De 1-2
20	Mk 15:21-47	De 3-4
21	Mk 16	De 5-6
22	Lu 1:1-25	De 7-9
23	Lu 1:26-56	De 10-11
24	Lu 1:57-80	De 12-14
25	Lu 2:1-24	De 15-17
26	Lu 2:25-52	De 18-20
27	Lu 3:1-18	De 21-22
28	Lu 3:19-38	De 23-25
29	Lu 4:1-15	De 26-27
30	Lu 4:16-44	De 28-29
31	Lu 5:1-16	De 30-31

April

Day	New Testament	Old Testament
1	Lu 5:17-39	De 32
2	Lu 6:1-26	De 33-34
3	Lu 6:27-49	Jos 1-4
4	Lu 7:1-17	Jos 5-7
5	Lu 7:18-50	Jos 8-9
6	Lu 8:1-18	Jos 10-12
7	Lu 8:19-39	Jos 13-14
8	Lu 8:40-56	Jos 15-16
9	Lu 9:1-27	Jos 17-18
10	Lu 9:28-45	Jos 19-20
11	Lu 9:46-62	Jos 21-22
12	Lu 10:1-20	Jos 23-24
13	Lu 10:21-42	Jud 1-2
14	Lu 11:1-28	Jud 3-4
15	Lu 11:29-54	Jud 5-6
16	Lu 12:1-21	Jud 7-8
17	Lu 12:22-40	Jud 9-10
18	Lu 12:41-59	Jud 11-13
19	Lu 13:1-17	Jud 14-16
20	Lu 13:18-35	Jud 17-19
21	Lu 14:1-14	Jud 20-21
22	Lu 14:15-35	Ruth 1-2
23	Lu 15	Ruth 3-4
24	Lu 16	1Sa 1-3
25	Lu 17:1-19	1Sa 4-6
26	Lu 17:20-37	1Sa 7-9
27	Lu 18:1-17	1Sa 10-12
28	Lu 18:18-43	1Sa 13-14
29	Lu 19:1-27	1Sa 15-16
30	Lu 19:28-48	1Sa 17

May

Day	New Testament	Old Testament
1	Lu 20:1-26	1Sa 18-19
2	Lu 20:27-47	1Sa 20-22
3	Lu 21:1-24	1Sa 23-24
4	Lu 21:25-38	1Sa 25-26
5	Lu 22:1-23	1Sa 27-29
6	Lu 22:24-53	1Sa 30-31
7	Lu 22:54-71	2Sa 1-3
8	Lu 23:1-25	2Sa 4-6
9	Lu 23:26-56	2Sa 7-10
10	Lu 24:1-12	2Sa 11-12
11	Lu 24:13-35	2Sa 13-14
12	Lu 24:36-53	2Sa 15-16
13	Jn 1:1-34	2Sa 17-18
14	Jn 1:35-51	2Sa 19-20
15	Jn 2	2Sa 21-22
16	Jn 3:1-21	2Sa 23-24
17	Jn 3:22-36	1Ki 1
18	Jn 4:1-26	1Ki 2-3
19	Jn 4:27-54	1Ki 4-5
20	Jn 5:1-18	1Ki 6-7
21	Jn 5:19-47	1Ki 8
22	Jn 6:1-24	1Ki 9
23	Jn 6:25-51	1Ki 10-11
24	Jn 6:52-71	1Ki 12-13
25	Jn 7:1-24	1Ki 14-15
26	Jn 7:25-39	1Ki 16-17
27	Jn 7:40-53	1Ki 18-19
28	Jn 8:1-20	1Ki 20-21
29	Jn 8:21-47	1Ki 22
30	Jn 8:48-59	2Ki 1-3
31	Jn 9:1-12	2Ki 4-5

June

Day	New Testament	Old Testament
1	Jn 9:13-41	2Ki 6-7
2	Jn 10:1-21	2Ki 8-9
3	Jn 10:22-42	2Ki 10-11
4	Jn 11:1-27	2Ki 12-14
5	Jn 11:28-57	2Ki 15-16
6	Jn 12:1-26	2Ki 17
7	Jn 12:27-50	2Ki 18-19
8	Jn 13:1-20	2Ki 20-21
9	Jn 13:21-38	2Ki 22-23
10	Jn 14:1-14	2Ki 24-25
11	Jn 14:15-31	1Ch 1-2
12	Jn 15	1Ch 3-5
13	Jn 16	1Ch 6
14	Jn 17	1Ch 7-8
15	Jn 18:1-24	1Ch 9-10
16	Jn 18:25-40	1Ch 11-12
17	Jn 19:1-16	1Ch 13-15
18	Jn 19:17-42	1Ch 16-17
19	Jn 20:1-18	1Ch 18-19
20	Jn 20:19-31	1Ch 20-21
21	Jn 21	1Ch 22-23
22	Ac 1	1Ch 24-25
23	Ac 2:1-21	1Ch 26-27
24	Ac 2:22-47	1Ch 28-29
25	Ac 3	2Ch 1-3
26	Ac 4:1-22	2Ch 4-6
27	Ac 4:23-37	2Ch 7-8
28	Ac 5:1-16	2Ch 9-11
29	Ac 5:17-42	2Ch 12-14
30	Ac 6	2Ch 15-17

All scripture is given by inspiration of God, and is profitable for doctrine, for reproof, for correction, for instruction in righteousness... 2 Timothy 3:16

Finding and deciding on a Bible to read can be a daunting task. There are so many to choose from. When you go into a bookstore you really do not know where to start. Sometimes when you begin attending a church you discover that the people in that church all read the same kind of Bible and the preacher uses that same Bible when preaching the sermon each week.

The following is a list of the Bibles I have read and can recommend.

Translations.

The Revised Standard
New King James Version
New International Version
New Living Translation
The New English Bible

Commentary Bibles.

The Amplified Bible
The Ryrie Study Bible
The Story NIV
The Message
The Chronological Study Bible
The Zondervan NIV Study Bible
The Quest Study Bible

Addiction Study Bibles.

The Freedom in Christ Bible
The Celebrate Recovery Bible

If you are inclined to do exhaustive study I would recommend.

Strong's Concordance
Mathew Henry commentary
William Barclay's commentary

As you begin a life of reading scripture it is a good idea to work out a schedule of reading. I think it is important to read and pray daily. Everyone is different when it comes to reading scripture. It works better for me to do my reading in the morning. Some would rather read in the evening and that is fine. Just pick a time and stick to it.

I find mornings to work better for me because I start the day putting scripture in my mind. I think it puts me in a better frame of mind the whole day. There is something to be said for giving God the first part of the day. We really should put Him first in everything we do.

Chapter 4
Scripture Memorization

There are several reasons I think it is important to memorize scripture. One is to help me not sin. I love the scripture verse Psalms 119: 11.

"I Have hidden your word in my heart that I might not sin against you."

In this scripture the psalmist is struggling with what we all struggle with, <u>sin</u>. I think when he says, "I have hidden your word in my heart" , he means he has read it enough that he knows it by heart. We know that sin begins with temptation.

The psalmist realizes when he is being tempted by Satan, he can recall a scripture to help himself overcome the temptation

James 1:13-15 says.

"When tempted, no one should say, "God is tempting me." For God cannot be tempted by evil, nor does he tempt anyone; but each person is tempted when they are dragged away by their own evil desire and enticed. Then, after desire has conceived, it gives birth to sin; and sin, when it is full-grown, gives birth to death."

.

The best way for me to illustrate this is a story about Jesus. After He was baptized by John in the Jordan River, Jesus was led out into the wilderness. While He was in the wilderness He fasted for forty days and nights. Maybe He was preparing himself for the ministry that He would be doing for the next three years and to ultimately die on the cross. I believe Satan waited till Jesus was at His weakest point from fasting and came to tempt Him. But all three times Satan tempted Jesus He responded by quoting scripture.

This is all recorded in Matthew 4:1-11.

"Then Jesus was led by the Spirit into the wilderness to be tempted by the devil. After fasting forty days and forty nights, he was hungry. The tempter came to him and said, "If you are the Son of God, tell these stones to become bread." Jesus answered, "It is written: 'Man shall not live on bread alone, but on every word that comes from the mouth of God.'"
Then the devil took him to the holy city and had him stand on the highest point of the temple. "If you are the Son of God," he said, "throw yourself down. For it is written: "He will command his angels concerning you, and they will lift you up in their hands, so that you will not strike your foot against a stone." Jesus answered him, "It is also written: 'Do not put the Lord your God to the test.'"

Again, the devil took him to an exceedingly high mountain and showed him all the kingdoms of the world and their splendor. "All this I will give you," he said, "if you will bow down and worship me." Jesus said to him, "Away from me, Satan! For it is written: 'Worship the Lord your God and serve him only.'" Then the devil left him, and angels came and attended him."

I remember well a sermon that one of my favorite preachers (Bob Russell) gave at Southeast Christian Church. It was on this passage and he used 3 points as follows.

If Jesus was tempted, so will we.
Jesus overcame, so can we.
Jesus used scripture as His compass, so should we.

My first exposure to scripture memorizing was when I was a discipling guide using a set of booklets called Operation Timothy. When you taught or were a student in this program you memorized a verse each week. By the end of the program you had 12 scripture's memorized. When I realized it was beneficial for me to memorize, I began memorizing several verses each year.

Sometimes as I was reading through the Bible I would come across a verse that just stood out to me.

Often when I was listening to the minister preach his sermon at church, he would share a scripture that I felt led to memorize. It is funny, now when I am listening to a message, there is almost always one or more of the scripture's the preacher uses that I have memorized. It is always a blessing to me that as the minister says the scripture I too am saying it in my head. It helps me to be more dialed into what he is saying and seems to mean more to me.

The following is my list of memorized scriptures and the reason I share them with you.

Books of the Bible

Old Testament
(Monday, Wednesday, Friday)

Gen 1:1-2 Ex 34:6-7 Joshua 1:8 Joshua 24:15
1Chr 4:10 2Chr 7:14 Ps 1:1-3 Ps 8:1-5 Ps 20:7
Ps 23 Ps 30:5 Ps 34:8 Ps 37:4 Ps 51:1-19 Ps
91:1 Ps 119:11 & 105 Ps 139:1-24 Prov 3:5-6
Prov 14:12 Prov 15:1&22 Prov 16:18 Prov 27:1
Isa 1:18-19 Isa 5:20-21 Isa 26:3 Isa 40:8 & 28-31
Isa 44:2 Isa 55:6&8-9 Isa 57:1 Jer 1:5 Jer 9:23-
24 Jer 17:9 Jer 29:11-13 Jer 31:33-34 Jer 33:3
Ezek 22:30 Nah 1:7 Mal 3:8-10

New Testament
(Tuesday, Thursday, Friday)

Mat 5:1-12 Mat 6:9-13 Mat 7:7 Mat 10:32 Mat 11:28-30 Mat 20: 18-20 Mat 28: 18-20 Mark 8:36-37 John 1:1&14 John 3:16 John 3:30 John 6:35 John 8:31-32,44 John 10:10 John 11:25-26 John 13:34-35 John 14:6 John 15:13 John 16:33 John 20:3 Acts 1:8 Acts 2:38-40 Acts 4:12 Rom 1:16&20 Rom 3:10&23 Rom 5:8&18 Rom 6:23 Rom 8:1 Rom 8:26-28&31&37-39 Rom 10:9-10&13 Rom 12:1-2 1Cor.1:18 1Cor 2:9 1Cor 10:13 1Cor 13:1-13 1Cor 15:19 2Cor 5:17 2Cor 7:10 2Cor 4:7-9&16-18 2 Cor 10:3-5 2 Cor 8:9 Gal 2:20 Gal 5:22-23 Eph 2:8-9 Eph 3:14-20 Eph 6:10-18 Phil 1:6 Phil 1:21 Phil 2:3 Phil 2:9-11 Phil 3:10-14 Phil 4:5-7&13 Col 1:16 Col 2:8 1Thess 2-8 1Thess 4:13-14 1Thess 5:16-18 1Tim 2:3-4 2Tim 2:2&15 2Tim 3:16-17 Heb 2:3 Heb 4:12 & 15-16 Heb 9:27 Heb 11:1&6 Heb 12:1-2 Heb 13:8 Jam 1:2-4&5-8&13-15&19 Jam 4:2&7 Jam 5:16 1Pet 1:15 1Pet 3:15 2Peter 1:21 2 Pet 3:8-9 1John 1:9 1 John 2:6 1 John 4:4 1 John 5:13-15 Rev. 3:20 Rev. 20:15 Rev 22:1-2

I do not share this list to impress the reader with my great ability to memorize. The fact is I have a hard time memorizing.

It has taken me forty years to memorize this list. I share it because I believe that these scriptures are some of the main ones we should know.

As I mentioned above you will almost always hear these used in sermons and Sunday school lessons. If you wanted to hide the Word in your heart, that you might not sin against God, many of these are good ones.

I want to share how I taught myself to memorize. I write out the scripture I am memorizing on an index card. I will memorize one line at a time. I will carry the index card in my pocket and take it out throughout the day when I have a chance. I will say the line I am working on ten times in a row. By doing this I am burning it into my brain just like burning something onto a computer CD. When I can say the line without any trouble then I move onto the next line.

I also decided early on it was so hard to memorize a scripture, that once I had it memorized, I did not want to forget it. I began to dedicate a part of my devotion time each morning for repeating my memory verses.

You notice in my list that it is separated into Old Testament and New Testament. The list got so long that I needed to divide it up. Now I repeat Old Testament scriptures on Monday, Wednesday, Friday, and New Testament scriptures on Tuesday, Thursday, Saturday.

You will notice at the beginning of the list, (Books of the Bible) which I repeat before I do the Old Testament verses. I felt led to memorize the names of the books of the Bible. One thing it does is save you the time of going to the index to find the location of the book you are looking for. For instance, when you are in church, Sunday school or a Bible study and you need to turn to a certain scripture, it becomes much easier.

I taught myself an easy way to do this. If you decide to read completely through the Bible you can try my method. You start out reading the first book which is Genesis. Each day as you begin reading say the name of the book you are reading a couple of times, which in this case is Genesis. When you get to the second book of Exodus start out each day saying Genesis Exodus a couple of times. Keep doing this. When you get to the fifth book Deuteronomy, you will be saying Genesis, Exodus, Leviticus, Numbers, Deuteronomy. Do this till you get to the end of the Bible and you will have all the books memorized. It will take a year, but it is well worth the effort.

I want to spend some time looking at special memory verses and why they are important to me. I think the first verse that you ever hear and probably the one that most church attendees will remember and know is,

John 3:16.

"For God so loved the world that he gave his one and only Son, that whoever believes in him shall not perish but have eternal life."

This verse is the very essence of the Gospel. It sums up what we must do to be saved. That is to believe there is a God who loves us and that He gave His only Son so that we could have eternal life.

In the same way that John 3:16 is the most well-known scripture in the New Testament, the 23rd Psalm is the most well-known scripture in the Old Testament. It is almost always used at funerals because it is a scripture that gives us comfort and strength in challenging times.

Psalm 23: 1-6

"The Lord is my shepherd; I shall not want. He makes me lie down in green pastures, He leads me beside still waters, He restores my soul. He guides me on path
righteousness for his name's sake. Even though I walk through the valley of the shadow of death, I will fear no evil, for you are with me; your rod and your staff, they comfort me.
You prepare a table before me in the presence of my enemies.

You anoint my head with oil, my cup overflows. surely goodness and mercy will follow me all the days of my life, and I will dwell in the house of the Lord forever."

I would like to introduce you to the Roman Road. It consists of five memory verses that can be used as an evangelism tool. You might find yourself in a situation where you are talking to someone and feel led to discuss salvation with them. If you do not have a Bible or anything to reference with, you can use the Roman Road. I have done it and it works fine. First I would share with them what God has done for you, and then I would share each of these five scriptures and what they mean.

Romans 3:10

"There is no one righteous, not even one."

Romans 3:23

"for all have sinned and fall short of the glory of God"

Romans 5:8

"But God demonstrates his own love for us in this: While we were still sinners, Christ died for us."

Romans 6:23

"For the wages of sin is death, but the gift of God is eternal life in Christ Jesus our Lord."

Romans 8:1

"Therefore, there is now no condemnation for those who are in Christ Jesus."

I have always loved the 51st Psalm. It was written by the great King David who was a man after God's own heart. David wrote this Psalm when he was feeling remorse and guilt after he had done something very evil. He had not gone off to a battle with his men. While the men were out fighting he was looking off his roof and spotted Bathsheba, one of the men's wife. She was bathing on the roof below him and she was incredibly beautiful. His was overcome by lust which led to him having an affair with her and getting her pregnant. It also led to him having her husband, Uriah, killed on the battlefield so he could marry her.

I often have felt like David because of sin in my life. When I came across this scripture and realized what it meant, I just had to put it in my heart.

51st Psalm.

"Have mercy on me, O God, according to your unfailing love, according to your great compassion. Blot out my transgressions. Wash away all my iniquity and cleanse me from my sin. For I know my transgressions, and my sin is always before me. Against you, you only, have I sinned and done what is evil in your sight; so, you are right in your verdict and justified when you judge. Surely I was sinful at birth, sinful from the time my mother conceived me. Yet you desired faithfulness even in the womb. you taught me wisdom in that secret place. Cleanse me with hyssop, and I will be clean.
wash me, and I will be whiter than snow. Let me hear joy and gladness; let the bones you have crushed rejoice. Hide your face from my sins and blot out all my iniquity.
Create in me a pure heart, O God, and renew a steadfast spirit within me.
Do not cast me from your presence or take your Holy Spirit from me. Restore to me the joy of your salvation and grant me a willing spirit, to sustain me. Then I will teach transgressors your ways, so that sinners will turn back to you. Deliver me from the guilt of bloodshed, O God, you who are God my Savior, and my tongue will sing of your righteousness. Open my lips, Lord, and my mouth will declare your praise. You do not delight in sacrifice, or I would bring it; you do not take pleasure in burnt offerings.

My sacrifice, O God, is a broken spirit; a broken and contrite heart you, God, will not despise. May it please you to prosper Zion, to build up the walls of Jerusalem.
Then you will delight in the sacrifices of the righteous, in burnt offerings offered whole.
then bulls will be offered on your altar."

Another favorite scripture is the one we call the love Chapter. When you want to understand God's love or share that love with others this scripture defines it.

1st Corinthians 13: 1-13

"If I speak in the tongues of men or of angels, but do not have love, I am only a resounding gong or a clanging cymbal. If I have the gift of prophecy and can fathom all mysteries and all knowledge, and if I have a faith that can move mountains, but do not have love, I am nothing. If I give all I possess to the poor and give over my body to hardship that I may boast, but do not have love, I gain nothing. Love is patient, love is kind. It does not envy, it does not boast, it is not proud. It does not dishonor others, it is not self-seeking, it is not easily angered, it keeps no record of wrongs. Love does not delight in evil but rejoices with the truth. It always protects, always trusts, always hopes, always perseveres. Love never fails.

Where there are prophecies, they will cease; where there are tongues, they will be stilled; where there is knowledge, it will pass away. For now, we know in part and we prophesy in part, but when completeness comes, what is in part disappears. When I was a child, I spoke like a child, I thought like a child, I reasoned like a child. When I became a man, I put the ways of childhood behind me. For now, we see only a reflection as in a mirror; then we shall see face to face. Now I know in part; then I shall know fully, even as I am fully known.

And now these three remain: faith, hope and love. But the greatest of these is love."

Maybe one of the most important scriptures in the Bible is the very first verse.

Genesis 1:1

"In the beginning God created the Heavens and the earth."

The one thing that separates Christians from the rest of humanity is that they have made Jesus their Lord and Savior. The greatest obstacle we encounter in that process is *God created*. It is so hard for us to get that in our mind. Every person I have known that refused to believe in God had at least one thing in common. They could not believe that God created them.

When you examine the expanse of the universe and the complexity of all that is in it, to say that it "just happened" or "evolved" requires more faith than to believe that God created it. God truly did create a wonderful universe, and he is worthy of our praise.

Why did God choose to create the universe and all that is in it? God is love, and love is best expressed toward something or someone else—so God created the world and people as an expression of his love. We must accept that God did create it all and He did it because he loves us.

Well the truth is that I could pick every one of the scriptures I have memorized and give a good reason why it is so important, but that would be another book.

I hope that you will decide to make this discipline a part of your life. I do not think you would ever be sorry you did. Yes, it is hard in the beginning, but over time it gets easier and it is so rewarding.

I also hope that memorizing scripture will bring as much joy and sense of accomplishment to you as it has to me.

Chapter 5
Church Attendance

In this chapter I will be talking about the Church, the meaning of the Church, how it came about, and what the Bible has to say about it. I will also talk about the importance of attending church regularly.

I mentioned in chapter two that one of the ways I knew God's spirit had come to live in me was the desire I had to attend church. Isn't it funny that I had gone my whole life and not thought about church until I accepted Christ as my Lord and Savior? I think it is just something that happens to each of us as we become a member of the Kingdom of God.

Let us go back and review the Kingdom of God. As we talked about in chapter one there is the kingdom of this world and the Kingdom of God. Those who have asked Jesus to be their Lord and Savior and committed their life to Him are now children of God and a part of the Kingdom of God. Those who have not become part of God's kingdom still belong to the kingdom of this world and are a part of Satan's family. I know this sounds harsh; however, it is a reality, and it is what the Bible teaches. Again, the Bible teaches there is no neutral. Jesus said you are either with me or against me.

The Pharisees asked Jesus when God's Kingdom would come, not knowing that it had already arrived. Unlike any earthly kingdom, the Kingdom of God has no geographical boundaries. Instead, it begins with the work of God's Spirit in people's lives and in relationships. I think to understand the Church we must understand the Kingdom of God. We then can realize the Church, much like the Kingdom of God, is more than just buildings, institutions, or programs.

We drive down the street and we see a beautiful cathedral with a steeple and a cross. We think "what a church". But is that really the Church? In the recent Covid19 pandemic we have learned that the Church is much more than a building. Restrictions were put in place to protect us that did not allow us to gather in a church building. Most groups found creative ways to do church. Thanks to modern technology arrangements were made for worship to be live streamed into people's homes. Some chose to gather in homes and watch the live streams together.

I have a friend Ed Berry who is the minister at Henry Christian Church in New Castle, Kentucky. After having gone through a battle with the virus himself, his church decided to do what some others did, and have drive-in services for many months. They built a platform in the parking lot and folks stayed in their cars to participate in worship.

The early church met in homes. I am talking about shortly after Christ had left earth. This was partly because they had not yet started building special places for the sole purpose of gathering, but also they were having to meet in secret because of persecution. In fact, even today, 2000 years later, there are people all over the world having to meet in secret because of persecution.

If I had to describe in what the church is to me, I would say it is the place where, we who are a part of the Kingdom of God, along with those who are searching for answers, meet together to worship, pray to God, partake in the Lord's Supper, receive teaching about God, and do Kingdom work. That statement probably does not do justice to describing the Church.

The Church can be defined as public worship of God or a religious service in a place of meeting. It can also be defined as the whole body of Christian believers, that is Christendom.

In the New Testament Jesus makes a statement that has become the foundation of the Church today.

Mathew 16: 13-20.

When Jesus came to the region of Caesarea Philippi, he asked his disciples, "Who do people say the Son of Man is?" They replied, "Some say John the Baptist; others say Elijah; and still others, Jeremiah or one of the prophets."

"But what about you?" he asked. "Who do you say I am?" Simon Peter answered, "You are the Messiah, the Son of the living God."

Jesus replied, "Blessed are you, Simon son of Jonah, for this was not revealed to you by flesh and blood, but by my Father in heaven. And I tell you that you are Peter, and on this rock I will build my church, and the gates of Hades will not overcome it.

Peter confessed Jesus as divine and as the promised and long-awaited Messiah. If Jesus were to ask you this question today, how would you answer? Is he your Lord and Messiah?

The rock on which Jesus would build his church has been identified as either; (1) Jesus himself (and his work of salvation by dying for us on the cross); (2) Peter (the first great leader in the church at Jerusalem); or (3) the confession of faith that Peter gave and that all subsequent true believers would give.

I lean toward (3) the confession of faith. I believe the foundation of the Church today is the confession that every Christian makes when they become a believer, that Jesus Christ is their Lord and Savior.

We see Christ Followers called Christians for the first time in the New Testament at the church in Antioch.

Acts 11:25-26.

Then Barnabas went to Tarsus to look for Saul, and when he found him, he brought him to Antioch.

So, for a whole year Barnabas and Saul met with the church and taught great numbers of people. The disciples were called Christians first at Antioch.

At this point I want to move quickly to where we are today with the Church. I must tell you there are thousands of books written about what has happened with the Church in the 2000 years since Jesus and His followers formed it.

While the New Testament books were being written in the 1st century AD. the Church was forming. During the 2nd century the Church took on the name of Catholic. Eventually because of being in the Roman empire it took the name of Roman Catholic. For the next 1400 years not a lot changed other than we see the two major groups distinguish themselves separately. First the Eastern Orthodox and later the Church of England. Around 1500 AD we see a major change in the church, sparked by what was called the Protestant Reformation. The reformation was brought on by great men of God like John Calvin who did not agree with some of the teachings of the Catholic Church as well as the politics that were playing out in the Church. Large denominations began to form like Baptist, Methodist, and Presbyterian spurred on by men like Calvin, Wesley, and Knox.

We find ourselves today with many choices when it comes to attending church. Basically, you choose between Catholic, Protestant, and smaller splinter groups that claim no alignment with either.

I would like to spend some time talking about how to choose a church. When I realized I needed to begin attending church, I began going with my wife to a Cumberland Presbyterian church. It may happen that way for you as well. You may be led to go with your parents, another family member, or a friend.

For many Christ Followers there comes a time when you realize it is important for the church you attend to have a believe system that aligns with your own,

When My wife and I were older, we would find ourselves living away from home. We would want to attend church and would go on the internet to search for an Evangelical Christian Church. When we found one that we might like, we would look at their Statement of Faith and what they believed to make sure it lined up with our beliefs. Some of those beliefs are as follows;

God is Creator and Ruler of the universe. There is one God in three persons: Father, Son, and Holy Spirit. We believe that God is the Creator and Sustainer of all things. He is Holy and Righteous. The only way to have an authentic relationship with God is through Jesus Christ.

We believe that God the Father holds all the attributes of God while exercising a unique role in the triune God.
The Godhead is in agreement with the role of each: God as Father, Son as Sacrifice, and Spirit as Power.

He is the father of Jesus Christ, by the power of the Holy Spirit, and yet still one with both as God. The Father adopts believers into relationship with Him as he prunes/disciplines believers to strengthen them for His glory.

Jesus Christ is the Son of God. He is co-equal with the Father as God. Jesus lived a sinless human life and offered himself as the perfect sacrifice for the sins of all people by dying on the cross. He arose from the dead after three days to demonstrate His power over sin and death. He ascended to Heaven's glory and will return again someday.

The Holy Spirit is equal with the Father and the Son as God. He makes us aware of our need to follow Jesus Christ as our Lord and Savior. He gives us guidance and leadership on a daily basis so we can obey God's Word and do what is right. He gives each of us spiritual gifts for the purpose of serving the Body of Christ. We seek to live under His control in all situations.

The Bible is God's Word to us. It was written by human authors, under the supernatural guidance of the Holy Spirit. It is the supreme source of truth for Christian beliefs and living. Because it is inspired by God, it is the truth which points us to Jesus and governs our thinking and lives. Where it speaks we listen and obey.

We believe that humanity, created by God, willfully sinned, and as a result is lost and without hope apart from Jesus Christ.

Salvation is a free gift of God. The death, burial and resurrection of Christ is the work which saves us. We place our faith in that and then act that faith out in the way we live. Every person has sinned, but every person can also be forgiven and saved by Christ. When we are baptized, through faith in that work of God in Christ, our sins are forgiven, we are sealed by the Spirit and begin living out our faith.

The church is the Body of Christ on earth, empowered by the Holy Spirit to continue the task of leading others to faith in Christ and teaching followers of Christ to obey and serve Him. Involvement in a local church is critical to individual growth, fellowship, and support for life's day-to-day challenges.

People were created to exist forever. We will either exist eternally separated from God by sin, or eternally with God through the forgiveness of our sin. To be eternally separated from God is Hell. To be eternally with God is eternal life. Heaven and Hell are real places of eternal existence.

There are also some practical things to look at when choosing a church. Do we feel comfortable with the style of worship? Do we enjoy and learn from the preaching? Does the church have a Sunday School or small group program that we can fit into? Does it have a youth program that our children can enjoy? Is there opportunity for us to become an active member and serve using the gifts that God has given us?

Probably the most important thing we can do when going through this process is to pray and ask God for guidance!

Now that we have discussed how to choose a church I want to talk about what the bible says about church attendance.

Acts 20:7.

"On the first day of the week we came together to break bread. Since Paul was ready to leave the next day, he talked to them and kept on speaking until midnight."

Acts 2:42.

"They devoted themselves to the apostles' teaching and to fellowship, to the breaking of bread and to prayer."

Acts 2:46.

"With one accord they continued to meet daily in the temple courts and to break bread from house to house, sharing their meals with gladness and sincerity of heart."

Ephesians 1:22–23.

"And He put all things in subjection under His feet and gave Him as head over all things to the church, which is His body, the fullness of Him who fills all in all."

Hebrews 10:24-2.

"And let us consider how we may spur one another on toward love and good deeds, not giving up meeting together, as some are in the habit of doing, but encouraging one another—and all the more as you see the Day approaching."

We see in the verse above Paul telling us not to give up meeting together.
We read all through the New Testament, from the time Jesus began to have followers, up to and after His death and resurrection, they were gathering.

Sometimes large crowds would gather in remote places, sometimes just a few in a home, this was the beginning of the Church referred to as the Body of Christ.

I would like to share some final thoughts as we finish this chapter on church attendance. Many times, I have heard people say, somewhat reluctantly, that when they were children their family was in church whenever the doors were open. I do not think it is a bad thing that children are encouraged to attend church. However, as we get older we must make our own decision concerning church. I am not sure that feeling guilty is the ideal motive for going to church. Nor should our motive be things such as networking for business or finding a social life.

I have also heard several people say you do not have to attend church to be a Christian. This is true. I know there are many reasons that someone may take that position. Maybe they have been hurt by the Church or its members, or maybe they feel like the Church is full of hypocrites. I can tell you no local church is perfect. The fact is Christians make mistakes and sometimes so does the local church.

When we read the descriptions of the early church—the miracles, the sharing and generosity, the fellowship—we may wish we could have been a part of this "perfect" church.

The early church had problems just as we do today. No church has ever been or will ever be perfect until Jesus and his followers are united at his second coming. All churches have problems. If your church's shortcomings distress you, ask yourself, would a perfect church allow me to be a member? Do what you can to make your church better. A church does not have to be perfect to be faithful to Jesus.

Church is our best opportunity to gather for God's glory. If we are not being drawn in that direction we might need to do a heart check.

I think that wanting to attend church should come from something deep inside us. There should be a new thing going on in us after we commit to the Lord. It should be a yearning in us to have a deeper relationship with the Lord. It comes from God's Spirit that now lives in us.

I have come to a point that Sunday is the most important day of the week for me. To go to church, to have a midday meal, and to relax the rest of the day, sets the tone for the week to follow.

After hardly ever missing church for many years, I have only been able to attend a few Sundays for the last 14 months. First because of having to have a double lung transplant and then because of the Coronavirus. It has been miserable for me. Just in the past few weeks we have been able to attend with some strict guidelines. I cannot tell you how happy it has made me.

To be able to worship, sing the old hymns, take communion, and listen to great preaching, has made me feel like I have died and gone to heaven.

My prayer is that you will want to make church attendance one of your disciplines. I hope that you will search out and find a local church where you fit in. I pray that you will find the same joy I have found for the last forty years being part of the Church, the Body of Christ.

Chapter 6
Giving

I have often heard it said that the closest thing to a person's heart is their money. I understand why it is sometimes hard for people to give money to things like charity and church. We work hard for our money and there are so many ways to be scammed these days. I have also heard it said that the church is always wanting money for something or all the church wants is your money. I suppose that these thoughts about giving to the church spring from the same place that produces the thoughts of not going to church because of being hurt or because it is full of hypocrites. So where do these thoughts come from? No doubt in some cases they are warranted because we know that the local church is not a perfect institution filled with perfect people. However, we should be careful of the things we say about the universal Church, the Body of Christ.

I wonder if what really stirs these thoughts is Satan doing his best work of keeping God's children off balance and distracted?

One thing I have learned over the years about the Church is that it is much like life, in that, it is what we make it. Have I seen some challenges in the local church? Yes, however I can say without any hesitation that the benefits of belonging to and attending church have far outweighed the challenges.

I have heard some say they are not getting anything out of church. I have come to believe that what we get out of church relates to what we put in it.

And so, it goes with giving. The truth is that what we give is a small portion of what we have been given. Jesus said in Luke 12:48.

"From everyone who has been given much, much will be demanded; and from the one who has been entrusted with much, much more will be asked."

I think most people, like myself, begin putting something in the basket when they first start attending church. But there should become a time when we discover tithing. For my wife and I it happened several years after we had been attending regularly. I cannot really say what caused us to begin the discipline of giving because it has been so long ago. All I know is a light went off for both of us about the same time. I am sure we had probably just heard a sermon about giving.

There are two things I can say about our life of tithing. First, it was hard in the beginning. We were already barely making it and not at all sure how we could get by. Secondly, since we began tithing our life has never been the same.

I have never felt comfortable talking about God prospering us because of what we have given. There are so many who have given everything and suffered or died for their faith. I can say that prior to tithing we lived week to week and after a few years of tithing it was not like that at all. I think part of that equation is, when you know that your tithe comes first, you learn to be more careful with your spending. I refer to that as living in God's economy.

Not many years after we had started tithing personally I felt a tug on my heart that we should start tithing in our businesses. It was not long until I started seeing the results and was amazed. I think about what Paul said in 2nd Corinthians 9: 6-11.

"Remember this: Whoever sows sparingly will also reap sparingly, and whoever sows generously will also reap generously. Each of you should give what you have decided in your heart to give, not reluctantly or under compulsion, for God loves a cheerful giver. And God is able to bless you abundantly, so that in all things at all times, having all that you need, you will abound in every good work. As it is written: "They have freely scattered their gifts to the poor; their righteousness endures forever." Now he who supplies seed to the sower and bread for food will also supply and increase your store of seed and will enlarge the harvest of your righteousness. You will be enriched in every way so that you can be generous on every occasion, and through us your generosity will result in thanksgiving to God."

What is Paul teaching us here about giving? First I think he is saying we should not give out of guilt or haste. We should feel good about what we give. There is no doubt in my mind that if we pray and ask God what we should give, He will put in our mind and heart what it should be. I think Paul is also saying that as we give God will make it easier to give. It is like salvation, when we ask Him to come into our heart, He comes in. We make a step in His direction and He makes a step in ours. I do not think He will ever force His way into our heart, nor will He force us to give.

I must be careful when talking about this. I can never take my eye off the target. We do not give for what we can get. We give because we are instructed to. Again, what we give is a small portion of what we have been given. What we have is not ours to start with. Without God we have nothing. Everything we have is His. He just allows us to be the caretaker. The sooner we learn this the easier life gets.

Psalm 50:10

"For every animal of the forest is mine, and the cattle on a thousand hills.
I know every bird in the mountains, and the insects in the fields are mine. If I were hungry I would not tell you, for the world is mine, and all that is in it."

Now let us see what the Bible teaches about tithing. First we should understand what tithing means. The word tithe literally means tenth in the Hebrew language. The Old Testament was written in Hebrew. We learn that the early men of God gave back to Him a portion of what He had given them. So, tithing becomes the act of giving back to God ten percent of all He has blessed us with. We see tithing talked about from the beginning to the end of the Old Testament. The first I see of tithing is in the first book of the Bible.

Genesis 14:18–20.

"Then Melchizedek, king of Salem brought out bread and wine. He was priest of God Most High, and he blessed Abram, saying, "Blessed be Abram by God Most High, Creator of heaven and earth. And praise be to God Most High, who delivered your enemies into your hand". Then Abram gave him a tenth of everything".

Genesis 28:16–22.

"Then Jacob awoke from his sleep and said, "Surely the Lord is in this place, and I did not know it". And he was afraid and said, "How awesome is this place! This is none other than the house of God, and this is the gate of heaven". So early in the morning Jacob took the stone that he had put under his head and set it up for a pillar and poured oil on the top of it. He called the name of that place Bethel, but the name

of the city was Luz at first. Then Jacob made a vow, saying, "If God will be with me and will keep me in this way that I go, and will give me bread to eat and clothing to wear, so that I come again to my father's house in peace, then the Lord shall be my God, and this stone, which I have set up for a pillar, shall be God's house. And of all that you give me I will give a full tenth to you".

I have always loved this story about Jacob called the "Dream at Bethel". On one of his journeys he ends up at Bethel. He lays his head down on a rock to sleep. While he is asleep he has a dream. In the dream he sees angels ascending and descending on a stairwell that reached to heaven. There have been famous paintings made of this scene. Above the stairs stood the Lord who said to him that this land would be his and his descendants. His descendants would be like the dust of the earth. All the people on earth would be blessed through him. Then Jacob said, "of all that you give me I will give a full tenth to you."

Interesting that he said a "full tenth." Years ago, I figured out that if I gave my tithe before taxes I ended up with the same amount then if I gave after taxes. The only difference is that if I gave before taxes the church got a little more and Uncle Sam (the government) got a little less and that was ok with Uncle Sam.

The tithe became part of the Mosaic law.

It was used to support the Temple, the Levites (priests), and to help the poor. When you think about it, that is what much of it is used for even today.

Not only do we see the tithe mentioned in the first five books (the Pentateuch), we also see it talked about in many of the other books like the historic books such as Chronicles, the poetic books like proverbs, the minor prophets like Amos and Nehemiah, all the way up to the last book of the Old Testament, Malachi.

Leviticus 27:30.

" 'A tithe of everything from the land, whether grain from the soil or fruit from the trees, belongs to the Lord; it is holy to the Lord"

Numbers 18:26.

"Speak to the Levites and say to them: 'When you receive from the Israelites the tithe I give you as your inheritance, you must present a tenth of that tithe as the Lord's offering."

Deuteronomy 14:22.
"Be sure to set aside a tenth of all that your fields produce each year."

2nd Chronicles 31:12.

"Then they faithfully brought in the contributions, tithes and dedicated gifts. Konaniah, a Levite, was the overseer in charge of these things, and his brother Shimei was next in rank."

Amos 4:4.

"Go to Bethel and sin; go to Gilgal and sin yet more. Bring your sacrifices every morning, your tithes every three years."

Nehemiah 13:11-12.

"So, I rebuked the officials and asked them, "Why is the house of God neglected?" Then I called them together and stationed them at their posts. All Judah brought the tithes of grain, new wine and olive oil into the storerooms."

Proverbs 3: 9-10.

"Honor the Lord with your wealth, with the first fruits of all your crops; then your barns will be filled to overflowing, and your vats will brim over with new wine."

I have always found it interesting that God used the last chapters of the Old Testament to tell us a few of the ways we break covenant with Him, one of which is withholding our tithe. It makes me think that tithing must have been especially important to Him.

Malachi 3: 8-10.

"Will a mere mortal rob God? Yet you rob me. "But you ask, 'How are we robbing you?' In tithes and offerings. You are under a curse—your whole nation—because you are robbing me. Bring the whole tithe into the storehouse, that there may be food in my house. Test me in this," says the Lord Almighty, "and see if I will not throw open the floodgates of heaven and pour out so much blessing that there will not be room enough to store it."

The only other place I see God tell us to test Him is in the New Testament book of Romans.

Romans 12: 1-2.

"Therefore, I urge you, brothers, and sisters, in view of God's mercy, to offer your bodies as a living sacrifice, holy and pleasing to God—this is your true and proper worship. Do not conform to the pattern of this world but be transformed by the renewing of your mind. Then you will be able to test and approve what God's will is—his good, pleasing and perfect will."

Tithing and offering ourselves as living sacrifices were so important to God that He instructs us to test Him in these areas of our life. Both are a part of our worship of Him.

What does the New Testament say about tithing?

In Matthew 23:23 Jesus condemns the Pharisees for tithing and ignoring the more important issues of justice, mercy, and faith:

"Woe to you, teachers of the law and Pharisees, you hypocrites! You give a tenth of your spices—mint, dill, and cumin. But you have neglected the more important matters of the law—justice, mercy, and faithfulness. You should have practiced the latter, without neglecting the former."

Mark tells an interesting story about Jesus.

Mark 12: 41-44.

"Jesus sat down opposite the place where the offerings were put and watched the crowd putting their money into the temple treasury. Many rich people threw in large amounts. But a poor widow came and put in two very small copper coins, worth only a fraction of a penny.

Calling his disciples to him, Jesus said, "I tell you the truth, this poor widow has put more into the treasury than all the others. They all gave out of their wealth; but she, out of her poverty, put in everything— all she had to live on."

Jesus understood that even though this widow gave a small amount compared to the others, her heart was more giving because she gave a larger percentage of what she had than all the others. This verse is also interesting because this widow gave *all she had to live on.*

There are many people today who say they cannot afford to give but this woman realized she could not afford not to give. Much like this widow, we cannot afford not to tithe.

I like what Jesus says in the Sermon on the Mount.

Matthew 6: 19-21.

"Do not store up for yourselves treasures on earth, where moths and vermin destroy, and where thieves break in and steal. But store up for yourselves treasures in heaven, where moths and vermin do not destroy, and where thieves do not break in steal. For where your treasure is, there your heart will be also."

What are our treasures? Certainly, a big part of them is our money. Here Jesus is teaching us that all our investments here on earth can be taken from us, but when we give to God's work it is eternal. These eternal investments help to do things like further God's Kingdom here on earth and help the poor.

Should we save money? I think we should, but I am not sure our savings should come before our responsibility to God. In fact, my experience has been that our savings have been made available because of us fulfilling our responsibility to God.

Overall, the New Testament is not as specific as the Old Testament when it comes to the tithe. One of my modern-day heroes of the faith is Billy Graham. He is one who advocates that the tithe is a carryover from the Old Testament. There are others who would argue against that idea. I tend to side with Dr. Graham and the Pastors I have served under who taught that tithing is a part of our stewardship.

There is no doubt that Jesus was teaching that His Followers should give. I think He was encouraging them to give more than just a tithe. Read what Jesus said to one of His followers in Mathew 18:18-22.

"A certain ruler asked him, "Good teacher, what must I do to inherit eternal life?" "Why do you call me good?"

Jesus answered. "No one is good—except God alone. You know the commandments: 'You shall not commit adultery, you shall not murder, you shall not steal, you shall not give false testimony, honor your father and mother." "All these I have kept since I was a boy," he said. When Jesus heard this, he said to him, "You still lack one thing. Sell everything you have and give to the poor, and you will have treasure in heaven. Then come, follow me." When he heard this, he became very sad, because he was very wealthy. Jesus looked at him and said, "How hard it is for the rich to enter the kingdom of God!"

We certainly see in the book of Acts that the leaders of the church, like Peter and Paul, were encouraging Christ followers to give all that they could. They were selling everything and laying the money at the feet of the Apostles to help all those in need.

Acts 4: 32-35.

"All the believers were one in heart and mind. No one claimed that any of their possessions was their own, but they shared everything they had. With great power the apostles continued to testify to the resurrection of the Lord Jesus. And God's grace was so powerfully at work in them all that there were no needy persons among them.

For from time to time those who owned land or houses sold them, brought the money from the sales, and put it at the apostles' feet, and it was distributed to anyone who had need."

Again, Paul shows us how serious he was about giving in the book of 1st Corinthians 16:1-2.

"Now about the collection for the Lord's people: Do what I told the Galatian churches to do. On the first day of every week, each one of you should set aside a sum of money in keeping with your income, saving it up, so that when I come no collections will have to be made."

I would like to close out this chapter on tithing (giving) with a parable that Jesus told.

Mathew 25:14-30.

"Again, it will be like a man going on a journey, who called his servants and entrusted his wealth to them. To one he gave five bags of gold, to another two bags, and to another one bag, each according to his ability. Then he went on his journey. The man who had received five bags of gold went at once and put his money to work and gained five bags more. So also, the one with two bags of gold gained two more. But the man who had received one bag went off, dug a hole in the ground and hid his master's money.

"After a long time, the master of those servants returned and settled accounts with them. The man who had received five bags of gold brought the other five. 'Master,' he said, 'you entrusted me with five bags of gold. See, I have gained five more.' "His master replied, 'Well done, good and faithful servant! You have been faithful with a few things; I will put you in charge of many things. Come and share your master's happiness!' "The man with two bags of gold also came. 'Master,' he said, 'you entrusted me with two bags of gold; see, I have gained two more.' "His master replied, 'Well done, good and faithful servant! You have been faithful with a few things; I will put you in charge of many things. Come and share your master's happiness!' "Then the man who had received one bag of gold came. 'Master,' he said, 'I knew that you are a hard man, harvesting where you have not sown and gathering where you have not scattered seed. So, I was afraid and went out and hid your gold in the ground. See, here is what belongs to you.' "His master replied, 'You wicked, lazy servant! So, you knew that I harvest where I have not sown and gather where I have not scattered seed? Well then, you should have put my money on deposit with the bankers, so that when I returned I would have received it back with interest. " 'So, take the bag of gold from him and give it to the one who has ten bags. For whoever has will be given more, and they will have an abundance. Whoever does not have, even what they have will be taken from them.

And throw that worthless servant outside, into the darkness, where there will be weeping and gnashing of teeth.'

The master divided the money among his servants according to their abilities. No one received more or less than he could handle. If he failed in his assignment, his excuse could not be that he was overwhelmed. Failure would indicate only laziness or hatred toward the master. The bags of silver represent any kind of resource we are given. God gives us time, gifts, and other resources according to our abilities, and he expects us to invest them wisely until he returns. We are responsible for using well what God has given us. The issue is not how much we have but how well we use what we have. If God truly is our Master, we must obey him willingly.

As I mentioned earlier our time, abilities, and money are not ours in the first place—we are caretakers, not owners.

I hope that if you have not already done so you will discover the joy of giving? It is one of the most satisfying experiences in the Christian life. It really is better to give than to receive.

May I encourage you to become sensitive to this matter of Christian tithing/giving.

Chapter 7
Serving

There comes a point in our walk with Christ when we need to start thinking about serving. After we have accepted Him as our Lord and Savior, after we have begun a prayer life, began reading scripture, began attending church, began giving, somewhere in all of that we should begin to feel the calling to the next level. I think that level is servanthood. It is the heart of discipleship. We learn that Jesus Himself set the example by becoming a servant to those around Him and taught His disciples that they too were to become servants. I would like to begin by sharing a parable that Jesus shared recorded in the book of Mathew.

Mathew 25: 31-36.

"When the Son of Man comes in his glory, and all the angels with him, he will sit on his glorious throne. All the nations will be gathered before him, and he will separate the people one from another as a shepherd separates the sheep from the goats. He will put the sheep on his right and the goats on his left.
"Then the King will say to those on his right, 'Come, you who are blessed by my Father; take your inheritance, the kingdom prepared for you since the creation of the world.

For I was hungry and you gave me something to eat, I was thirsty and you gave me something to drink, I was a stranger and you invited me in, I needed clothes and you clothed me, I was sick and you looked after me, I was in prison and you came to visit me.'

"Then the righteous will answer him, 'Lord, when did we see you hungry and feed you, or thirsty and give you something to drink? When did we see you as a stranger and invite you in, or needing clothes and clothe you? When did we see you sick or in prison and go to visit you?'

"The King will reply, 'Truly I tell you, whatever you did for one of the least of these brothers and sisters of mine, you did for me.'

"Then he will say to those on his left, 'Depart from me, you who are cursed, into the eternal fire prepared for the devil and his angels. For I was hungry and you gave me nothing to eat, I was thirsty and you gave me nothing to drink, I was a stranger and you did not invite me in, I needed clothes and you did not clothe me, I was sick and in prison and you did not look after me.'

"They also will answer, 'Lord, when did we see you hungry or thirsty or a stranger or needing clothes or sick or in prison, and did not help you?'

"He will reply, 'Truly I tell you, whatever you did not do for one of the least of these, you did not do for me.'

"Then they will go away to eternal punishment, but the righteous to eternal life."

This parable describes acts of mercy we all can do every day. These acts do not depend on wealth, ability, or intelligence; they are simple acts freely given and freely received. We have no excuse to neglect those who have deep needs, and we should not think that these responsibilities belong only to churches or the government. Jesus demands our personal involvement in caring for the needs of others.

Jesus teaches us in this parable that whatever we do or do not do to others it is as if we have done it to Him.

I am reminded of a story I once read about Francis of Assisi who was born in 1182 and established the Franciscan order of monks.

The story goes that one day, Francis was riding down the road and he saw a leper. He was terrified of getting the disease, so he quickly turned to go in the opposite direction. But as he turned, something stopped him. Francis remembered the story of Jesus healing a leper in the Bible, and he knew that he could not just walk away. Francis felt compassion for this leper who had not been touched in years. He imagined what it would be like to have no one to hug you when you are sad, or pat your back when you are sick, or shake your hand to say hello and he knew he could not simply walk away. Instead, Francis walked right over to the man, and kissed him! Then, Francis emptied his pockets and gave the leper all the money he had.

Some accounts of the story tell that during the embrace the lepers face turned into that of an angel. Other accounts tell that as Francis moved on he looked back, and the leper was no longer there.

We know this would be possible. An example is found in the book of Facts about an early church leader named Stephen.

Acts 6:8-15.

"Now Stephen, a man full of God's grace and power, performed great wonders and signs among the people. Opposition arose, however, from members of the Synagogue of the Freedmen (as it was called)—Jews of Cyrene and Alexandria as well as the provinces of Cilicia and Asia—who began to argue with Stephen. But they could not stand up against the wisdom the Spirit gave him as he spoke. Then they secretly persuaded some men to say, "We have heard Stephen speak blasphemous words against Moses and against God." So, they stirred up the people and the elders and the teachers of the law. They seized Stephen and brought him before the Sanhedrin. They produced false witnesses, who testified, "This fellow never stops speaking against this holy place and against the law. For we have heard him say that this Jesus of Nazareth will destroy this place and change the customs Moses handed down to us."

All who were sitting in the Sanhedrin looked intently at Stephen, and they saw that his face was like the face of an angel."

We read in Hebrews 13:2.

"Keep on loving one another as brothers and sisters. Do not forget to show hospitality to strangers, for by so doing some people have shown hospitality to angels without knowing it."

What I am trying to show in this parable of Jesus about the sheep and the goats, as well as the story of St Francis and the leper, is when we serve others we are serving Jesus.

So how do we get started serving? There is one thing for sure, you do not have to look far in this world to see a need. I want to spend some time talking about several kinds of service including serving our family, serving in the Church, serving in the community starting with our neighbors, and serving in para-ministry organizations.

Serving our family

Let us start with being a husband. How are you serving your wife? It took me many years to realize that my wife is my best friend. Do we treat our wives as our best friends? We should! And more than that she is our partner in life.

In most cases our wife manages our home, cooks our meals, meets most all our needs, takes care of us when we are ill, I could go on and on. Is there anyone on this earth that we should want to serve more? We should protect her at all costs. Sometimes we need to do the things she wants to do instead of always what we want. Sometimes we need to talk to her and listen to what she has to say. I must be careful about talking over my wife because I tend to do that. I learned how to do my own laundry, and some of the cooking. I learned how to help clean the house, especially my man cave. One thing I was guilty of for many years was coming home and taking out on my wife the frustrations I had with those I worked for or with. I did not have the guts to stand up to those problems, but I could come home and make my wife's life miserable. She never deserved that. I hope you will consider this and not fall into the same trap. Wives are also not the one who cause us to have a bad golf game or not catch any fish. Above all we should treat our wives with respect. All of this is the beginning of serving our wives.

Serving as a wife is much like that of the husband. We see in the beginning of the Bible the importance of a wife to a husband. Genesis 2:18.

"The Lord God said, "It is not good for the man to be alone. I will make a helper suitable for him."

The 31st chapter of Proverbs has much to say about the serving wife not only to her husband but to her whole family. I will share a few of the verses.

"A wife of noble character who can find. She is worth far more than rubies.
Her husband has full confidence in her and lacks nothing of value. She brings him good, not harm, all the days of her life...She gets up while it is still night; she provides food for her family and portions for her female servants...She sets about her work vigorously; her arms are strong for her tasks...She sees that her trading is profitable, and her lamp does not go out at night...She opens her arms to the poor and extends her hands to the needy...When it snows, she has no fear for her household; for all of them are clothed in scarlet...She is clothed with strength and dignity; she can laugh at the days to come...She speaks with wisdom, and faithful instruction is on her tongue...She watches over the affairs of her household and does not eat the bread of idleness...Her children arise and call her blessed; her husband also, and he praises her:

I am going to talk here about my own wife, whom I think has been a perfect example of a serving wife. I look back 50 years and see that in the beginning she was my girlfriend and lover. Over time she became my best friend. Now in our later years she has also become my caregiver through some pretty trying times which included a double lung transplant. Through all those years she had our children and took such great care of them. She worked many years outside the home only to get home from work and cook our meals, clean our house, wash our clothes, take the kids where they needed to go, pay the bills, and many other things. Honestly, I look back now and do not know how she did it. She had a servant's heart. I must believe it was mostly because she gave her heart to Jesus at an early age. I also think that she inherited much of what she did from watching her mother and grandmothers.

Are you a mother or father? How are you treating your children? The Bible has a lot to say on this. Probably one of the most used verses on this topic is.
Proverbs 22:6.

"Train up your children in the way they should go, and even when they are old they will not depart from it."

I have come to learn that the biggest part of serving involves an investment of time. Teaching our children involves time and patience. I wish I could go back and raise my children with the same attitude I have today. I was too selfish with my time when my children were growing up. My wife was so much better with that than I was. Now as a grandfather I try to do a little better job.

I had a church friend named Bobby Watson. He would take his daughter once a week to get a milkshake and just talk. I wish I had done that. The Bible has a lot to say about how we are to treat our children. One very popular verse is. Ephesians 6:4.

"Fathers, do not exasperate your children; instead, bring them up in the training and instruction of the Lord."

What does it mean to exasperate your children? To exasperate is to irritate or frustrate. The purpose of parental discipline should be to help children grow into mature adults and Christians, not to exasperate and provoke them to anger or discouragement. Parenting with love and discipline takes a lot of patience and understanding. Frustration and anger should not be causes for discipline. Instead, parents should act in love, wisely treating their children as Jesus would treat them. Parents must also be diligent to give them the instruction and encouragement that is vital to their upbringing. Do your children see you reading the Bible? Do you pray for and with them daily? Do you take them to church and let them see how important church is to you? Can they see the difference Christ makes in your life?

We serve our children by being a big part of their life. There are so many ways we do that. Being involved in their schooling. Taking part in their hobbies and activities such as sports.

Maybe the most important thing is talking to them. There are different stages in their lives that we need to have certain serious talks with them such as sex and drugs. We should have a relationship with them that allows them to be comfortable coming to us to discuss anything that is on their mind. We must ask ourselves the question, "would we rather our children discuss these things with us or a stranger?"

Serving the Church

Our serving the Church begins with attending and being a part of worship.
Often in recent times we hear church attendees make comments like "I'm just not getting anything out of church." Many church attenders have evolved into an attitude of wanting to be entertained. An important part of having a good experience in church is being an eager participant. Get to the service a few minutes early and take time to meditate and focus on worship. Then sing like you mean it, pray like you mean it, listen attentively to the sermon, take communion in a spirit of reverence and repentance thanking Jesus for His sacrifice. It is so important for the Holy Spirit to be present in the church service and each of us who attend play a part in that happening. We should leave the church service saying to ourselves "today it has been good to be in the house of the Lord!"
Invest in the work of the Church. We all have some gifts that can be put to good use. You may be asked to be an Elder or Deacon.

Maybe your gift would be serving communion or being a greeter. If you are uncomfortable in roles like that, there are so many other things that need to be done, like preparing the church for worship, taking care of the church building and grounds. You might have the ability to teach Sunday school or lead small groups. One of my gifts has always been to visit and pray with those who are hurting. There is always a need for people willing to come alongside with others who are suffering, searching, or who need to be discipled.

Mathew 9:37 says.

"Then he said to his disciples, "The harvest is plentiful, but the workers are few."

There is so much to do in the Church. I know in the beginning it is hard to get plugged in. I also know that if you are serious and will pray about its God will provide a way. Seek out someone to talk with. Go to the Pastor and tell them you would like to help but do not know how to get started.

Serving our neighbors and community

It is hard for me to think about serving my neighbor without recalling the story of the Good Samaritan.

It is one that is always taught to children in Sunday school. The story is recorded in Luke 10:25-37.

"On one occasion an expert in the law stood up to test Jesus. "Teacher," he asked, "what must I do to inherit eternal life?

"What is written in the Law?" he replied. "How do you read it?" He answered, "Love the Lord your God with all your heart and with all your soul and with all your strength and with all your mind'; and 'Love your neighbor as yourself." "You have answered correctly," Jesus replied. "Do this and you will live." But he wanted to justify himself, so he asked Jesus, "And who is my neighbor?"

In reply Jesus said: "A man was going down from Jerusalem to Jericho, when he was attacked by robbers. They stripped him of his clothes, beat him and went away, leaving him half dead. A priest happened to be going down the same road, and when he saw the man, he passed by on the other side. So too, a Levite, when he came to the place and saw him, passed by on the other side. But a Samaritan, as he traveled, came where the man was; and when he saw him, he took pity on him. He went to him and bandaged his wounds, pouring on oil and wine. Then he put the man on his own donkey, brought him to an inn and took care of him. The next day he took out two denarii and gave them to the innkeeper. 'Look after him,' he said, 'and when I return, I will reimburse you for any extra expense you may have.'

"Which of these three do you think was a neighbor to the man who fell into the hands of robbers?" *The expert in the law replied, "The one who had mercy on him."*

Jesus told him, "Go and do likewise."

A couple of things in this story gets my attention. First, you should know that the Samaritan was the least likely to be the good neighbor. Samaritans were a group of despised people in that time and that region. It makes me feel like we do not have any excuses for not helping our neighbor. Second, Jesus said *"go and do likewise."* I believe that in this context Jesus is telling all His followers, including each of us, go and do likewise.

Recently after a serious surgery my neighbor, Dennis Hampton, mowed my yard a few times while I recovered. There are just so many ways we can serve our neighbors. We have another neighbor, Mary Stratton, who from time to time brings us a fresh hot loaf of sourdough bread she has just gotten out of the oven. These things mean so much to us. Not long ago I had a neighbor whose mailbox was knocked over. He is a Vietnam veteran and because of injuries has a hard time dealing with something like that. Myself, another neighbor Ryan Lipkey, and my grandson took the time to replace the broken post and fix it up like new. I was so blessed because it gave me an opportunity to work and talk with my neighbor and my grandson as well as put a smile on the face of a man who has been through so much that he doesn't get to smile a lot.

I see people come home from work, pull in the garage, shut the door behind them before they get out of the car and that is all you ever see them. We should know our neighbors well enough to be able to check in on them from time to time to see how they are. You would be surprised how much joy comes from getting to know your neighbors and stopping to talk to them when you see them out. Sometimes a friendly face with a word of encouragement can go a long way in somebody's life.

If we know there has been illness or tragedy we should offer our help. Something as simple as helping clean up tree limbs after a bad storm can or picking up a trash can and trash when the wind has blown it over can mean so much to a neighbor.

I spoke earlier about my next-door neighbor's father suffers from pulmonary fibrosis. It is a disease I am familiar with because I too have it. I ultimately had to have a double lung transplant. I felt led to begin spending time with him because we could talk about things others could not relate to. He is homebound now on full time oxygen. Several times a month I try to spend the afternoon with him. We eat and talk for several hours each time. I try to let him talk as much as he will. I cannot tell you how much of a blessing it has been to me and I know it means a great deal to my neighbor and her family.

Serving in the community goes beyond what we do in our neighborhood and there are so many ways to serve. Some of us are wired to be a part of civic organizations such as the Kiwanis or Rotary club or maybe the town council or parks board. Others may find working with youth to be their calling. There is such a need of Christian men and women to help in things like youth sports, scouting, Big Brother, and Big Sister programs, after school tutoring, etc. One thing I enjoyed doing was serving at our local food pantry. Helping to distribute food to the poor in the community is something that does not take a huge commitment, usually one day a week, but can be so rewarding.

Serving Para-ministry organizations

Para-ministries are faith-based organizations that work outside the Church and across denominations to engage in social welfare and evangelism. In most cases the work is voluntary, however there are usually some paid staff to run and manage the organization. You usually start out doing hands on work to help accomplish the mission that has been established. You may be asked to step up to be a board member or even serve on the staff. I have had the privilege to be able to go on short term mission trips over the years with one of the many mission outreach groups. The following are a list of the organizations I worked with over 35 years.

I do not share this list to be boastful in any way, but to give you an idea of some ministries that are available and are good ones in the area I live in.

Wayside Christian Mission, Louisville (specializes in offering food and shelter to the homeless as well as help with addiction)

Youth for Christ, Louisville, Ky. (works with youth of all ages to help them with life)

Go International, Wilmore, Ky (arranges and facilitates short term mission projects in third world countries)

Cornerstone Christian School, Shelbyville, Ky (provides education K1 through 12th grade)

Awake Ministries, Shelbyville Ky (Provides food for needy families, backpack program for school children, veterans assistance, addiction rehabilitation)

Jesus taught that we should follow His example and have a servant's heart. There is so much to do around us if we are willing to reach out. I hope you will spend some time in prayer and ask God to give you direction in this area of your life. I will guarantee that you will be blessed and will be a blessing to others.

Ask yourself, "how can I be a blessing to someone today?"

Chapter 8
How to use our disciplines in troubled times

In the introduction I talked about how we were going through some challenges such as the Coronavirus, political strife, and civil unrest, all of which has caused much division in our country and lives.

I personally have been through the greatest battle of my life in the last 4 years. Beginning with learning I had a terminal illness. I had to fight that disease for three years and then spent another year going through a double lung transplant. Three months after my recovery I began having issues with my stomach. I had to have three surgery's over an eight-month period that included having 12" of my colon removed and wearing a colostomy bag.

There is a card game called blackjack. When playing blackjack, if you have a good hand, you can choose to make a move called "doubling down." I heard a preacher say recently, as he was talking about these problems we are dealing with, that it was time for Christians to double down on their faith. I like that idea. It was really what got me through the suffering and trials I mentioned above.

What does it mean to "double down" in our faith?

I think it means pray like you have never prayed before, read scripture like you have never read before, attend church like you have never attended before, find other Christ followers to come along beside you in prayer, stick as close to your family as you can, and do not be too proud to ask for help.

I have also heard several preachers recently say things like "there are times when we need to be silent and listen" or "It is times like this when we as God's children need to act like God's children and be the light that shines in the darkness." There are times when we need to choose our words carefully. We should ask ourselves questions like.

"Am I going to be a peacemaker or a peace breaker?"

Jesus, who was the Prince of peace, said in Matthew 5:9

"Blessed are the peacemakers for they shall be called the children of God."

I think back just a few years when it was popular to wear a rubber wrist bracelet that said WWJD. It stood for "What would Jesus do?

Now looking back over many years, I can share what these disciplines have meant to and done for me. When we say the word discipline it seems to stir an idea of work. In some ways that is true. You do have to work at a discipline.

However, over time I found that doing these things did not seem like work at all. I did not begin doing them all a one time.

When I asked Jesus to come into my heart I began to read the Bible.

Next I realized that I was praying more. It was several years before I began forming and using a prayer journal.

Along the way I started attending church regularly.

Somewhere in those early years I began memorizing a few scriptures.

Eventually my wife and I realized we should be tithing.

Finally, I began to feel the call to servanthood.

It is true that we are creatures of habit. Sometime over the years the disciplines I was doing became part of my routine. Much like when we get up in the morning, we brush our teeth, wash our face, fix our coffee, etc.

Surprisingly today I do not really think about doing these disciplines because they have become a part of my life. In fact, I would say the biggest part of my life. I never have a day where I think of these disciplines being a burden in any way. On the contrary, if I have a morning that I cannot have my alone time with the Lord it bothers me. If I was not able to attend church, for instance when Covid19 had our church closed, it bothered me. When I am not doing something to serve others it bothers me.

As these disciplines have become so much a part of my life, it has made it easier to get through the tough times as well as enjoy and cherish the good times. I hope the reader will consider trying one or all of them. I feel certain it will change your life, just as it has mine and many other Christian friends.

In closing I would like to leave you with two of my favorite verses,

2 Timothy 2:15;

"Do your best to present yourself to God as one approved, a worker who has no need to be ashamed, rightly handling the word of truth."

Matthew 28:18-20

"Then Jesus came to them and said, "All authority in heaven and on earth has been given to me. Therefore, go and make disciples of all nations, baptizing them in the name of the Father and of the Son and of the Holy Spirit, and teaching them to obey everything I have commanded you. And surely I am with you always, to the very end of the age."

Appendix 1
Chapter memory and study verses

Chapter 1

Romans 3:23
"all have sinned and fallen short of the glory of God."

Romans 6:23
"For the wages of sin is death, but the gift of God is eternal life in Christ Jesus our Lord."

Romans 5:8
"God demonstrated His love for us in this: While we were yet sinners, Christ died for us."

John 14:6
"I am the way the truth and the life, no one comes to the father except through

Chapter 2

Eph 2:8-9
"For It was by grace that you were saved through faith - and this is not of yourselves, it is a gift of God - not of works lest any man should boast."

2 Corinthians 10:3-5
"For though we live in the world, we do not wage war as the world does.

The weapons we fight with are not the weapons of the world. On the contrary, they have divine power to demolish strongholds. We demolish arguments and every pretension thought that sets itself up against the knowledge of God, and we take captive every thought to make it obedient to Christ."

Acts 2:38-39
"Repent and be baptized in the name of Jesus Christ, for the remission of your sins, and you will receive the gift of the Holy Spirit."

Chapter 3

Joshua 1:8
"Keep this Book of the Law always on your lips; meditate on it day and night, so that you may be careful to do everything written in it. Then you will be prosperous and successful."

2nd Timothy 3:16-17
"All Scripture is God-breathed and is useful for teaching, rebuking, correcting and training in righteousness, so that the servant of God may be thoroughly equipped for every good work."

2nd Peter 1:21
"Prophecy did not have its origin in the will of man, but it was handed down to men of God as they were carried along by the Holy Spirit."

Chapter 4

Psalms 119: 11
"I Have hidden your word in my heart that I might not sin against you."

John 3:16
"For God so loved the world, that He gave His only begotten Son, that whosoever believeth in Him, shall not perish but have everlasting life."

23rd Psalm
"The Lord is my shepherd; I shall not want.
He makes me lie down in green pastures,
he leads me beside still waters,
He restores my soul.
He guides me along the paths of righteousness,
for his name's sake.
Even though I walk
through the valley of the shadow of death,
I will fear no evil,
for you are with me.
your rod and your staff,
they comfort me.
You prepare a table before me
in the presence of my enemies.
You anoint my head with oil.
my cup overflows.
Surely your goodness and mercy will follow me
all the days of my life,
and I will dwell in the house of the Lord Forever."

Chapter 5

<u>Psalm 84:10</u>

"For a day in your courts is better than a thousand elsewhere. I would rather be a doorkeeper in the house of my God than dwell in the tents of wickedness."

Psalm 122:1

"I was glad when they said to me, "Let us go to the house of the Lord!"

Chapter 6

Luke 12:48.
"From everyone who has been given much, much will be demanded; and from the one who has been entrusted with much, much will be asked."

Romans 12: 1-2
"Therefore, I urge you, brothers, and sisters, in view of God's mercy, to offer your bodies as a living sacrifice, holy and pleasing to God—this is your true and proper worship.

Do not conform to the pattern of this world but be transformed by the renewing of your mind. Then you will be able to test and approve what God's will is— his good, pleasing and perfect will."

Chapter 7

Mathew 9:37 says.
"Then he said to his disciples, "The harvest is plentiful, but the workers are few."

Matthew 25:40
"The King will reply, 'Truly I tell you, whatever you did for one of the least of these brothers and sisters of mine, you did for me."

Proverbs 22:6
"Train up your children in the way they should go, and even when they are old they will not depart from it."

Chapter 8

Matthew 5:9
"Blessed are the peacemakers for they shall be called the children of God."

2 Timothy 2:15
"Do your best to present yourself to God as one approved, a worker who has no need to be ashamed, rightly handling the word of truth."

Appendix 2
Chapter Questions

Chapter 1

Why did God create us?

How can we know God when we cannot see Him?

What causes us to be separated from God?

What did God do to make it possible for us to become part of His family?

How do we respond to what God did for us so we can spend eternity with Him?

Chapter 2

What is prayer?

Why do we pray?

What part of Himself did God make available to us, so we know how to pray and live the life He wants us to live?

How does God speak to us?

What is a prayer journal?

Chapter 3

Why is it important to read the Bible?

When men wrote the Bible, how did they know what to say?

What are the 2 main parts of the Bible and how are they different?

What is a Bible lectionary or study plan?

Chapter 4

What are some reasons to memorize scriptures?

Who was the best example in the Bible of repeating scriptures when tempted? Can you think of an example?

What is a good method of memorizing scriptures?

What is the Roman Road? Can you name the verses?

Chapter 5

What is the Kingdom of God?

What is the Church?

How did Jesus tell Peter He would build His church? What did He mean?

Why should we attend church?

Chapter 6

What does the word tithing mean?

Where do we see some early examples of tithing in the Bible? Can you name one?

How do we know that giving was a part of the New Testament Church?

What is the difference of treasures in heaven and treasures on earth?

Chapter 7

Who was the best example of someone who served others? Can you give an example?

What are some examples of ways we can be servants?

Chapter 8

How do we use our disciplines in times of trouble or suffering?

Made in the USA
Columbia, SC
31 December 2021